INSTAGRAM SECRETS

"The most dependable and consistent way to generate wealth is to turn advertising into profit."

Frank Kern, Legendary Internet Marketer

INSTAGRAM
SECRETS

The Underground Playbook To
Grow Your Following Fast,
Driving Massive Traffic &
Generating Predictable Profits

JEREMY MCGILVREY

First Edition

ISBN-13: 978-0692873953

ISBN-10: 0692873953

DEDICATION

To my son Tristan, who helped me realize how magical the miracle of life truly is.

To my son Thomas, everything I have and everything I will become was made possible because of you.

And to all the people who didn't believe in me. Thank you for the extra motivation.

CONTENTS

FOREWORD

Smartphone + Instagram = Gold Mine

When I first started on Instagram, it was nothing more than a way for me to add value to people's lives. I treated Instagram like a blog where I would share my story and experiences as an entrepreneur. I quickly realized that Instagram users were hungry for my content because it provided a combination of high-quality images, a feel of luxury, and a powerful message of inspiration and encouragement.

Little did I know I was setting myself up for the entrepreneurial journey of a lifetime. I honestly didn't know that it was possible to turn Instagram into a profitable business at the time. I was completely unaware of the massive money-making opportunity that was lying dormant within this mobile social media platform.

All of that changed when someone offered to pay me $25 to shoutout their Instagram page. It doesn't sound like much, but that one second in time changed the course of my life. Immediately, I doubled down and figured out what was working to grow my audience and what wasn't. I had already put in the hard work of consistently creating valuable content and building my following, but now it was time to take it to the next level.

From that point forward, I took Instagram serious and treated it like a real business that had the potential to make real profits. I began to form partnerships with some of the largest pages on Instagram and paid them to promote my Instagram page. I started posting high-quality content every few hours instead of only once or twice a day. I noticed that nobody else was using videos strategically, so I became the first person in my niche to post inspirational videos that would motivate people and encourage them to pursue their dreams. If there was ANYTHING that could increase my follower base and drive more traffic to my Instagram page, I was doing it.

As a result of my increased efforts over a 2-year time-frame, I was able to achieve the following:

- 2,300,000 followers on my verified Instagram page @Millionaire_Mentor

- Featured in Forbes and several other prominent publications

- Successfully launched multiple 6-figure and 7-figure businesses online

- Internationally recognized as one of the top affiliate marketers in the world

- Collected 350,000+ email leads using only my Instagram page

- Netted $2,000,000+ in profits through my Instagram page alone

All of this was possible because of two simple things that are unique to Instagram. The first is that you can drive traffic at speeds that will blow your mind. The second is that unlike other social media platforms, you have no limitations on what you can put on your promotions. That's why Instagram is a gold mine and a marketer's dream come true!

The best part about my achievements is that the actual steps to monetize my Instagram account and grow my following are rather easy to do. The trick is to actually FIND what the steps are, and then DO them consistently, day in and day out.

Unfortunately, there is a lot of misinformation out there and that makes it difficult to find the right steps. It's sad to see so many hard-working people on Instagram throw money at failed strategies that sound good but don't actually work.

I don't want you to make the mistake of trying to figure out how to succeed on Instagram by yourself. I've already discovered exactly what works and what doesn't work, and my results are a testament to this.

A secret to success in any area in life is to model the steps of people who are already successful, and building your Instagram business is no exception to this rule. I modeled the techniques that top Instagram Influencers used to become successful, and I managed to follow in their footsteps until I achieved the same results as they did. In some cases, I've even managed to surpass them.

In the same way that I modeled my strategies after

other successful people on Instagram, Jeremy modeled his Instagram strategies after mine.

When I first met Jeremy, I quickly realized that he and I shared the same lion-sized entrepreneurial ambitions. We developed a business relationship and I eventually taught him everything I knew about Instagram – all of my insights, my tips, my secrets, and my strategies for achieving success on the social media platform.

It was no surprise to me that Jeremy's growth on Instagram through his brand page @ElevateYourMindset exploded. He was able to collect email leads like I did and soon he was able to monetize his Instagram page. Eventually, he turned much of what I taught him into Instapro Academy, which is currently the best-selling Instagram training program in the world for teaching professional marketers how to use Instagram to generate predictable profits.

I was so impressed with Jeremy's rapid success that I decided to team up with him and offer regular webclasses that teach people how to succeed on Instagram. You can attend our next webclass by visiting: www. FreeIGTraining.com. Together, Jeremy and I are going to teach people all around the world about the power of Instagram so it can change their lives just like it has changed ours.

I firmly believe that Jeremy's book is the formula that people who are searching to make money online have been looking for. Throughout the 21 chapters he walks you step-by-step through the exact techniques and strategies that I personally used to net over $2,000,000 and become one of the top influencers on Instagram. He shows you how to do everything RIGHT so that you don't have to make the mistakes that I see other people making on Instagram on a daily basis. After you read this book you won't have to spend any more time doing things the wrong way. You will now be able to spend your valuable time focusing on the strategies that actually get results.

Instagram Secrets is going to teach you exactly how to capitalize on the incredible opportunity this social media platform offers online marketers. For example, you are going to learn how to create captivating photos and compelling captions in order to get Instagram users to stop scrolling through their newsfeeds and engage with your post. You are also going to learn how to develop relationships with Instagram Influencers because doing so on a regular basis will be key to your Instagram success. You will learn how to drive massive traffic to your website or sales funnel. And you will learn how to create irresistible offers that Instagram users can't refuse.

However, I want to make it clear that Instagram is NOT a "get rich quick" scheme. Building an Instagram business requires a lot of work and self-discipline especially at the beginning. You will likely not be able to monetize your page in the early stages and you will have to work very hard to build an audience and consistently provide value to them. There will be a lot of testing and strategic thinking that you have to do in order to solidify your niche and make yourself stand out from the rest of the competition.

You will not be able to passively read Instagram Secrets just once and make millions overnight. You may have to re-read certain chapters in this book until you've mastered the strategies Jeremy reveals to you. A smart way to increase your speed of success would be to read a strategy, implement it, and take notes on what went right and what you could have improved before you move on to the next strategy.

Currently, there is no other book about Instagram on the market that gives you time-tested advice from someone who has actually achieved consistent monetary success on Instagram. With this book in your hand, you will finally stop burning money on other social media platforms and start printing money on Instagram. You now have the opportunity to reap incredible profits and put yourself in a position to succeed on the hottest social media network that exists.

Building an Instagram business could finally be what gives you a true sense of purpose in life. It might allow you to achieve financial freedom at last. It could be that new opportunity you are looking for because your day job is sucking the life out of you.

No matter what your reasons are, it is important to hold on to them as you embark on your Instagram journey. Because those reasons will carry you through the difficult times and inspire you to work even harder during the good times.

So if you're ready, flip the page over and let Jeremy walk you through exactly how I was able to not only build an Instagram page that has millions of followers, but make millions of dollars and live life on my own terms.

Let's get started!

To your success and wealth on Instagram,

- Jason Stone, aka Millionaire Mentor

INTRODUCTION

12 Reasons Why Instagram Dominates Every Social Media Platform

Congratulations on purchasing a copy of this book! You have in your hands the only guide that you will ever need to achieve massive success on Instagram – both financially and influentially. With this comprehensive step-by-step playbook, the only reason you won't succeed will be a catastrophe where Instagram magically disappears overnight (and the likelihood of that happening is slim to none!).

It's hard for people to believe that you can really do wonders for your business and your brand with such a deceivingly simple social media platform. It took a mere two years to build Instagram's photo sharing app and its growth has become a marketers dream come true. Instagram was eventually sold to Facebook for $1 billion, a testament to the incredible value and future that Instagram has as a social media platform. Today, Instagram is valued at more than $40 billion!

What makes Instagram unique is how incredibly simple it is in nature and in design. No annoying buttons, excessive features, sketchy links or intrusive pop-ups. You view a vertical gallery of beautifully taken photos while sharing your own photos with friends, fans and loved ones. Brand awareness, audience engagement, generating leads, increasing sales – all of this is possible on Instagram for anyone who is seeking to achieve these objectives for themselves and/or their business.

Instagram is a powerhouse for countless reasons – its ease of use and simplicity is remarkable, it has seamless features that keep users engaged and practically addicted. It provides people with a way to express themselves visually making the app a natural way to document and share your life with the world, or simply just people you know and care about. All of this, combined with the financial backing of a $400 Billion company like Facebook, Instagram is part of so many people's daily lives and it shows no signs of slowing down.

Instagram is one of the most powerful ways to express yourself, build a community and tap into a world of millions of people. In the hands of an entrepreneur, it can be an extremely valuable resource for building an empire of loyal fans and followers who can't wait to buy your products and services.

Do you want to drive traffic to your website or sales funnel? Instagram allows you to do that at speeds that will amaze you. Are you looking for a way to share the dream that's been placed in your heart with people around the world? Instagram can help you do that as well, at a very high level. How about adding something more personal and relatable to your content? Instagram gives you the ultimate power of storytelling through engaging photos, short videos and live streaming. It is the ultimate platform for providing people with an intimate look into your life and your business in real-time.

No other photo sharing application has experienced this kind of success and I firmly believe Instagram will continue to rise in power and scope for many years to come. Did I also mention that the Instagram app is FREE to anyone who has a smartphone?

Nike, Red Bull, Tiffany & Co. – you name it, they have all jumped on the Instagram train. More importantly, they have found ways to turn otherwise boring topics into highly visual stories that people can interact and engage with. There is always a way to make something more exciting, which is what you will need to do if you want to appeal to your audience. With Instagram, you'll get much more conversation going with share-worthy videos and stunning photos than a boring product on a display stand in your local store.

Don't believe me? Does it sound too good to be true? Listen to what Gary Vaynerchuk, CEO of Vaynermedia has to say about Instagram:

"Anybody right now who isn't spending a dispropor-
tional amount of time trying to figure out the hashtag
culture, the Instagram ad product, organic Instagram posting, working with Instagram Influencers is
making a huge mistake to not set their business up
properly in the 2018-2019 world. We haven't even
seen the real revenue come in from Instagram yet.
It's a beast. It is the current social network."

Why should you listen to Vaynerchuk? Not only is he
the world's biggest authority on social media, he also
has the uncanny ability of predicting which social media
platforms will rise and fall. He has both the experience
and results to stand by his claims. Many people will pay
nearly any dollar amount for just one piece of advice
from Vaynerchuk.

You need to understand that with your mobile phone
you possess the most valuable yet underutilized marketing tool in existence. Instagram will not provide
this extraordinary opportunity for long because other
people, especially marketers, will see how powerful this
social media platform is and soon everyone will be on
Instagram.

Here are 12 reasons why Instagram is dominating all
the other social media platforms:

1.   Instagram allows you to reach up to 100% of your
      followers, Facebook only allows you to reach
      about 6%

2. Instagram's engagement is amazing (likes, comments, shares, etc.) – 58 times more than Facebook and 120 times more than Twitter

3. Instagram is extremely easy to use – next to no learning curve

4. 2016: Instagram had 23% growth compared to 1.8% growth for Facebook, Twitter actually lost users

5. Instagram has equal distribution amongst iPhone and Android users

6. Instagram currently has 650-plus million active monthly users

7. Organic engagement has grown by 115% on Instagram – compared to a 63% decrease of organic engagement on Facebook

8. The average order is $65 on Instagram versus only $55 on Facebook

9. Instagram's growth rate continues to double every other smartphone app

10. Instagram is extremely efficient at deleting fake or spam accounts

11. 96% of marketers use Facebook, while 36% use Instagram (On Instagram you only have to compete with about a third of the marketers online)

12. The average Instagram account grows in followers by 16% per month (Nearly 200% per year)

Each bullet point in that list is a dream come true for any business or Influencer who wants to expand their reach and create another source of income. Why would a business not want to take advantage of the extraordinary opportunities Instagram gives us? It's baffling to see how many people make the conscious choice to dismiss Instagram as an effective marketing tool.

Here's the one thing you really need to get your mind around if you are going to achieve fast and long-term success on this hot social media platform:

Successful Instagram marketers do what 99.9% of people will not do. They do not treat it like something that can be hastily put together and updated without care or attention. Each and every element is carefully and purposefully engineered to achieve their goal: Improve and increase traffic, increase engagement, boost sales via higher conversions rates.

In this book, you will learn how to create your own strategy that defines you and your brand on Instagram. I'm going to teach you exactly how to create an extremely loyal and active community of followers that rely on you for massive value.

Fortunately, you are reading this book at a time where people have just started to figure out how Instagram can be leveraged for their benefit. In the not too distant future, Instagram will become saturated with people using the tactics and strategies I reveal in this book, and becoming a unique voice on the platform will become much more difficult. That's not taking into account the fact that Instagram will also go through several changes.

For instance: Instagram recently launched live video streaming. This feature allows you to connect with your followers in real-time. And the best part is, the moment you go live Instagram alerts all of your followers who are online and tells them to watch your stream. Another amazing feature Instagram released not long ago is their stories feature. This was Instagram's answer to Snapchat's "story". This feature allows you to upload photos and short videos to a separate news feed that appears behind your Instagram logo and at the top of each Instagram user's newsfeed that currently follows you. These features have been game-changers, and later in this book I am going to show you exactly how you can take full advantage of them to grow your reach and ultimately your brand.

This book will be regularly updated as Instagram continues to roll out more features because the last thing I want to do is release this book and completely forget about it. I want this book to be the only guide that you will ever need to grow your following and achieve massive success on Instagram. You should be able to succeed with nothing else other than the strategies, tactics and tools you learn in this playbook.

One of the biggest problems that I see in the Instagram marketing field is information overload. People try to read too many things from too many different sources and it leads to inaction and confusion. You can't tell the experts apart from the novices. The idea of becoming successful on Instagram starts to sound like a big waste of time. You get discouraged, give up and return to your old ways of marketing.

I want you to be able to trust the information in this book. This is not some theoretical framework that I came up with in my head that sounds great on paper. You possess information that I have personally used to achieve massive success on numerous Instagram accounts within multiple niches. I've purchased dozens of courses and spent a ton of money figuring out what does and doesn't work on Instagram.

Why is it so important to learn from someone who has actually implemented the strategies they teach? Because I believe that unless you sell dog food, or work at a funeral home, you should always be your own best customer. A lot of people are out there teaching strategies and techniques that they have never done themselves and will never do in their lifetime.

When I started posting images on my Instagram page @ElevateYourMindset there were struggles and there were numerous roadblocks, especially in the beginning. But I knew that people were making a lot of money on Instagram and I convinced myself that I could do the same thing too. Eventually, I figured out what worked and put everything I learned into this book. What was most surprising to me is that there are accounts that are much larger than mine yet still use these same techniques to grow their following and influence on Instagram to this day.

My primary Instagram page @ElevateYourMindset has a massive following and I'm making predictable profits from it on a daily basis. Currently, I don't do any other form of online advertising – my company and I are 100% on Instagram. So believe me when I say that I have the results to back up the information that I am going to teach you inside this book.

There's a saying that relates to my teaching style, which is: You can't do the fancy stuff until you master the fundamentals.

Once you master the fundamentals of successfully growing your Instagram following, you can focus on automating the process which will allow you to take your Instagram page to levels that you didn't think were possible. If you took away nothing else but this formula you would be very successful:

Fundamentals + Automation = Sustained Success

The fundamentals and the habit of consistently applying them day in and day out is what will make or break your marketing efforts on Instagram. You could completely skip the automation part and still do very well for yourself. Just remember, you cannot automate successfully if you are automating garbage!

This book is designed to help you master the fundamentals as quickly as possible. The act of automation is quite easy to set up once you know how to do it. I will show you exactly what needs to be done and the tools that are best suited for getting your marketing strategy on autopilot.

There will be a lot to cover, so don't feel guilty if you can't apply all of the techniques right away. It takes time before you find the best strategy that works for you and your business/brand. Focus on one fundamental at a time and truly master it before you move on to the next. Take as much time as you need – you're in this for the long haul, right?

As I just mentioned (it's worth repeating), you cannot do the fancy stuff (automate your Instagram account) until you master the fundamentals (set your Instagram page up correctly and sales funnel up properly). Most people immediately jump into the fancy stuff on Instagram and then wonder why they fail. It's almost always because they do not have the fundamentals down and that leads to them struggling, burning out and eventually quitting. I highly recommend that you ignore everything else you have heard about Instagram and use nothing else except the information in this book. You may find that you have to unlearn some beliefs that have sabotaged your progress on Instagram thus far, but trust me it will be well worth it.

Throughout this book, you will notice that I do not give out exact numbers for certain techniques. For example, you will not see me saying that implementing technique #24 will give you a 17% increase in engagement or using strategy #116 will increase your conversions on your sales funnel by 36%. I believe that when you do so, you are giving false promises to people because the cold hard truth is, everyone will achieve different results.

As you will see, there are numerous variables that need to be taken into account, and each one will have an effect on the engagement or lack of engagement that your Instagram post receives. Treat them as fundamental rules to follow and don't get too hung up on the exact numbers. The most important part of building your Instagram page is applying the basics that will eventually increase your engagement with your ideal audience over the long-term.

I'd like to make a quick disclaimer before we begin: Many of the strategies I used to grow my Instagram pages and make money on Instagram came from interviewing some of the top Instagram Influencers in my niche. I don't claim to have came up with all the techniques and strategies I reveal to you in this book. It's much like when Tony Robbins wrote the book: *Money Master The Game*. Tony is not the wealthiest person in the world. However, he did interview many of the wealthiest people in the world, got their secrets and compiled them into a comprehensive book that provided people with a strategy for generating wealth.

My primary objective is to give you time-tested advice that has worked for me, along with giving you information that I wish I had when I was first starting out. Information that would have saved me a lot of wasted time and money. Rather than make the mistakes I did, you can learn from my experience and shorten the time it will take for you to succeed on Instagram.

I would also like to mention that the results for each person who reads this book will vary. I am going to teach you exactly how I got 100,000 followers in under six months, but maybe for you it will take 7 or 8 months for you to hit the 100k mark. I can't speak for everyone – it will depend largely on your own efforts and the niche you choose.

With that being said, wouldn't you rather be at 90,000 followers in 6 months with a predictable revenue stream instead of a mere few thousand followers with no money? You will achieve far more success growing your Instagram following from the principles in this book than trying to figure it all out on your own like I did in the beginning. You will thank me six months from now when your Instagram page is growing like wildfire on autopilot and you're finally able to generate a predictable paycheck.

Please understand, growing your Instagram following and profiting from this platform requires consistent commitment and dedication. You will not get the results you are looking for if you are not willing to put in the work. In the beginning, you may experience situations where you find yourself disappointed with slow progress. You need to be relentlessly persistent in applying the fundamentals and working at building your Instagram page each and every day. Once you read through this entire book, it will be up to you to implement all the techniques and strategies I reveal. After you do so, then you will have to have the patience to allow your progress to compound over time.

Make sure that you read and understand each chapter before you move on to the next one. I know that I jam-packed this book with a ton of information, but that's only because I want to provide you with as much value as possible. You will quickly see that each strategy is connected to each other, with each new strategy building on what you learned previously. This is why I suggest you do not skip around in this book, because if you do things will likely get confusing and you won't have the context to understand why I advise you to do certain things in a certain way.

Even though using all of the advice in this book will leave you well-equipped for massive growth, just using one or two tips can make a big difference in your success on Instagram. If you are a newbie to Instagram, you can follow everything in chronological order. Seasoned veterans will view this book as a refresher of what they already know combined with some new insights that might be able to help them break through long-standing plateaus of growth that I see so many Instagram Influencers go through.

Everything in this book is well-explained – the psychology behind a typical Instagram user, the strategies

I've used that maximize my growth (and hindered it – remember I'm far from a perfect human being), how to track your follower growth in real-time and with accuracy, how to distinguish legitimate pages from fake or suspicious ones, and far more.

One final note: You need to really think about what you are looking to get out of Instagram:

- Why are you making an Instagram account in the first place?

- What are your goals (for follower growth and weekly revenue)?

- Do you already have an existing brand that you want to promote and grow?

- Are you willing to put in the time to create appealing images and visual content that delivers massive value to your followers?

- Do you have the energy, self-discipline and resources to follow each of the time-tested techniques and strategies that I give you in this book?

Sporadic posting (i.e. post 10 images on a single day of the month and do nothing else) and inconsistency will not fly here. If you are going to succeed on Instagram, you need to make a commitment to do something each and every day for your Instagram page (it's kinda like being a parent to a small child, you don't get sick days). You will have to hustle and grind for the first few months. There is no getting around that. But once you put the work in, things will become much easier and you will be able to set your sights on much larger goals. More followers, greater engagement, and predictable daily profits will be well within your reach.

If you are using multiple social media platforms and you are just getting started with Instagram, expect to re-direct most of your efforts to Instagram until you develop your following (unless you hire/outsource someone to do this for you). You will learn a lot about online audiences and how they operate throughout the 21 chapters in this book.

You will also receive a lot of real-world marketing experience, and that's something many companies will pay greatly for. Businesses and organizations of all sizes are willing to pay top dollar for people who possess the skills to help them reach an online audience where millions of potential customers can be found. If you have the skills and the know-how for building massive audiences on Instagram, you have a valuable skill set that can be added to your resume. It could even lead to a career in social media marketing, or at minimum, a side hustle where you can earn large sums of supplemental income.

If you are a business: This book is going to teach you exactly how to grow your Instagram following fast, generate massive traffic to your website or sales funnel, and how to collect targeted email leads faster than any other place on the entire Internet.

If you are not a business: Get ready to learn how your Instagram page can become a business and turned into a money making machine no matter what previous experience you may or may not have!

I hope you're ready to generate predictable profits

and experience massive growth and engagement on your Instagram page.

Let's dive in!

CHAPTER 1

The Instagram Environment: You Can't Play the Game If You Don't Know the Rules

Before we jump into the tips, tricks, secrets and strategies contained within this book, you need to understand exactly what you are dealing with when it comes to the Instagram environment. Otherwise, you will waste a lot of time trying to learn strategies that will not get you maximum results. You need to learn how Instagram operates before you can jump in and use the tactics outlined in this book.

Consider this a primer for those who are completely new to Instagram. Experts should read this as a brief refresher.

1. INSTAGRAM IS **99.9% MOBILE**

The overwhelming majority of Instagram users are accessing the app through their mobile device. It's far easier to use on a phone compared to the desktop application and this will not change anytime soon. Everything that you do needs to be done with the consideration of how it will be viewed and perceived on a mobile device. Don't assume that what you see is what everyone else sees. Make sure to view your adjustments and changes on the mobile app to see how they appear. This is far different from every other social media application where engagement is spread somewhat evenly amongst multiple platforms.

This also holds true for any sales copy you use on Instagram. With a limited amount of space, long form sales letters have no place on Instagram. Why? Because you have far less room (and time) to get your message across.

Here's another way to look at this: People are addicted to their phones and have a really hard time putting them down and your followers and customers are waiting to engage with content on Instagram that appeals to them. They are rapidly scrolling and browsing through all the posts on their newsfeeds so it is vital that you catch their attention immediately and deliver value the second they see your Instagram post. You don't have to worry about the .1% of people who use Instagram on their desktop computers because pretty much everyone these days is spending all of their time on their phones. A Pew Research study recently revealed, "Nearly 80% of social media time is spent on a mobile device."

On another note, everything on your website or sales

funnel, presuming you have one, needs to be fully optimized for mobile use, it has to be setup for easy viewing on a phone. If the website is not mobile optimized, you're basically throwing money down the drain.

Instagram's desktop version, is primarily used to control third-party applications and modify certain preferences. It doesn't serve much use outside of these two functions. In fact, the desktop version only came into the picture recently. To this day you still can't post to your Instagram account from the desktop version (unless you use one of the risky third party apps). This may sound like a downfall until you realize how astonishingly easy Instagram is to use on the go. This is what leads to the highly active user base (more than 650,000,000 monthly users) that you see on this incredibly hot social media platform.

2. HIGHLY VISUAL IS THE NAME OF THE GAME

Every single photo that you post needs to be high-quality, no ifs, ands or buts about it. In this day and age, people are expecting crisp and clean photos as a bare minimum. With the standard being higher than ever, you will quickly fall behind if you do not obey this vital rule.

By nature, humans are exceptionally visual creatures. We process visual information much faster than any other type of media and the majority of information processed by our brains is visual. Research has proven that we remember vivid imagery far better than anything else.

Instagram takes full advantage of this biological principle. In this book, you are going to learn how to leverage visuals to your advantage. When you apply the principles I teach you in chapter 7 for making crisp photos, your page will become eye candy to anyone who views it and as a result, you will attract more followers.

The takeaway is clear: You need to create highly visual content. Your Instagram posts need to be clean and well-designed. Those who think they can just slap random stuff together and call it content are the ones who burn out the fastest and end up broke.

3. MASSIVE COMMUNITIES ARE ALREADY ON INSTAGRAM

Although you will be creating your own community, you must understand that there are already huge groups of people that exist on Instagram within virtually every niche. You need to pinpoint exactly where they are and figure out how to tap into them. This is important to understand if you want to drive massive traffic to your Instagram page and grow your follower base extremely fast.

This all doesn't seem too complex, does it? That's how ridiculously simple the Instagram platform is. However, you need to apply laser focus in following and executing the strategies in this book with a complete understanding of the Instagram environment before you can effectively take advantage of the massive communities and utilize them to drive traffic, grow your own follower base and ultimately generate consistent and predictable profits.

Now that you know what to expect on this amazing platform, you are ready to begin setting up your Instagram profile.

CHAPTER 2

9 Steps To Creating the Perfect Instagram Name

If you already have an Instagram account you can skim through these first few paragraphs but be sure to carefully read the next section when I discuss choosing your Instagram name.

Setting up an Instagram account is very easy and should take you no more than a couple of seconds. Download the app to your mobile phone and open it up.

On the main screen, you will have the option to sign in with your Facebook login or use your email address. Choose one and move on.

You will be able to build out your profile with the following details:

- **Full name:** This is the name of your brand/business (or your personal name) spelled out in full (ex. Elevate Your Mindset)

- **Username:** After filling out the above, you will get an automatic suggestion for what your username should be. This is separate from your full name (ex. @ElevateYourMindset)

- **Password:** Make sure you choose something that is secure and easy to remember

- **Photo:** Use your logo or a picture of yourself if it's a personal page

Click on "Done", and you will immediately have access to the Instagram platform and your new Instagram account.

Don't worry about getting everything perfect right away. As you read through this book, you will learn exactly how to build your new or existing account into a powerhouse brand and begin attracting new followers with ease. This is simply the first step.

NAME: WHAT PEOPLE WILL CALL YOUR INSTAGRAM PAGE

The name you choose for your Instagram page is absolutely crucial. Your Instagram name is similar to a modern website domain name these days. When people search for you, it needs to be recognizable and pop up right away. The way you craft your name will determine a significant portion of your success on Instagram. Unless you're already a world-famous brand or a celebrity that everyone knows by name, people should read your name and immediately have a good idea of what your brand is about. This is the first step to maximizing your growth on Instagram. People will be disappointed or confused when they see content that does not match with your name. Everything: Promotions, shoutouts, etc. – will deliver subpar results if you get this wrong.

Sounds like common sense? It certainly does until you realize how many people will haphazardly jump into this process and fail at growing and profiting on Instagram before they even get started.

Don't rush this! You don't need to be a perfectionist but you want to take a good amount of time to come up with the right name. Ask friends, family, anybody that you trust. You are looking for their brutally honest first impression upon seeing and hearing your name.

Here are a couple of things to watch out for when you're choosing your Instagram name:

Pronunciation: It should be easy to say your name. No part of your name should be confusing at all.

Unique: Obviously, you can't use a username that has already been taken. You also want to avoid similarities to any other businesses or brands that are already on Instagram. Copyright infringement problems will come back to bite you when you begin growing your page in the near future.

Periods and/or Underscores: You might have to use these in order to create a unique name for yourself. Ideally you want to avoid using them at all but this might not be realistic. Limit your use of these, and never put two or more periods/underscores right beside one another. The reason for this is because it makes it harder for people to search for you and find your name. Google will treat "word1.word2.word3.word4" as four separate words, making the discovery of your page much more difficult.

Length: This should not be too long (the same goes for your Full Name). How long? Go to any page and look at who they are following. The full name AND the username should not be cut off at all. All this does is add ambiguity and confusion to potential followers who don't understand what your page is all about. Conciseness and clarity are key to a successful Instagram name – this is why you should take your time. Shorter names are easier to search for and may provide you with exclusivity.

Gender/Ethnicity/Religion: Keep these out of your name. Unless that is your specific niche, you are going to severely limit the potential size of your audience before you even begin. You have to respect what your followers want to see if you want to keep them around and engaged with your content and Instagram page.

Popular Names: Try to keep these out of your name (ex. Success, entrepreneur, billionaire, etc.). There are several huge Instagram accounts that dominate in these niches and you will be facing a steep uphill climb as you attempt to grow your following. A unique name will make your page much easier to discover when people are searching for you.

Relevancy: As stated earlier, you want your name to be relevant to the content you post. Use your niche's key word in the first part of your name and not the middle or last part of it. Enter the mind of a person who is searching for your niche: What is the FIRST thing they will type in the search field on the Instagram app? The keyword. If your word isn't there, it's going to get lost amongst the other search results. This is a simple way to utilize search engine optimization within the Instagram environment.

For example, when I launched my first Instagram page I chose the username @FSTRSuccess because I thought it was clever and easy to understand but I was dead wrong. Within just a few weeks I quickly realized I needed a username that aligned more with my brand and what I do. After I changed my username to @ElevateYourMindset I saw a dramatic increase in my follower growth. Now if you search either 'elevate' or 'mindset' my page comes up in the first handful of searches in a very crowded niche. Think long-term when it comes to the relevancy of your name and how it connects with your brand.

Similar to Your Website: If you don't have a website yet, try to set up a domain that matches or is very similar to your chosen Instagram username. You don't have to spend a lot of money on this and you can even have an email address that includes your Instagram username. From personal experience, I've noticed that contact@username.com provides the most clarity because people know exactly who they are reaching when they send an email. This email also provides superior results to something like a Gmail address, even if the username is included in that Gmail account (ex. username@gmail.com). With that said, Gmail might be the best option if you do not currently have a website or have secured a domain name.

Also, if enough people click on your website, which will be featured in your bio – (more on that later), you will eventually achieve a higher search rank on Google and you will find that people can discover you outside of the Instagram platform. You don't necessarily have to focus too much on this but as you grow you may find it beneficial. As great as Instagram is, a global brand is built off of multiple platforms through which will help you become far more accessible to people around the world.

Secured Across Multiple Platforms: This is more relevant towards those that want to expand their reach on multiple social media platforms (Facebook, Twitter, Snapchat, YouTube, etc). This ensures that your branding is simplified and unified. The only exception to this is that you want to keep your personal accounts separate from the accounts you use for businesses and influencing. Unless your model requires you to be an integral part of the page, you will lose followers if people see constant selfies of yourself and not the content that they want and expect to receive.

After some time and some brainstorming, you should have several names ready. Take them through the 9 criterias I've outlined until you have something that passes all of the tests. You're almost there!

Before you select your final Instagram username, you want to be clear about what you are building. Are you building your own personal page, something for your business, or a general page on Instagram that focuses on a specific niche? This will affect the name you choose and you may even have to go back through the previous criterias I laid out to ensure that your Instagram name passes all the tests.

THE 3 MOST COMMON TYPES OF INSTAGRAM ACCOUNTS

Personal: A personal account is one where people share highlights and exciting moments from their personal lives. Here, you can set up a compelling name that focuses around you (or your brand) and your life. For example, Gary Vaynerchuk has the username @garyvee. It's what he calls himself and everyone knows exactly who it is when they hear this nickname. You want that same kind of 'instant' recognition for yourself.

Business: A business page usually posts products and services for people to discover in the hopes of acquiring a new customer or client. In this context, your name needs to be attractive to your niche and so it must follow the above rules in order to attract your ideal customer or client to your Instagram page. At the same time, you also want something that immediately brings your own brand into light. Focus on the benefits of working with your brand and not necessarily the brand as a whole. This means that you want to avoid CO's, INC's, or LLC's in your name.

Niche Page: Also known as the passion page. The key here is to build a recognizable name that people can associate with your brand and your brand only. You want your name to encompass your niche AND provide a benefit or a meaning. People need to read your name and immediately know what you do. This is crucial for getting more followers to your Instagram page quickly – along with over time as well.

Now, I want to remind you that if you have plans to monetize your Instagram page, you need to choose a name that's already associated with a profitable niche. There's no point in creating your own market when you can tap into ones that are already developed through years of hard work. Becoming a pioneer on Instagram isn't the best way to accelerate your profits, model what works and don't attempt to reinvent the wheel.

Here is a small sample of the niches on Instagram that I know from experience are very powerful in influence and size. If your niche isn't listed below, you will have to do some research to see if it is realistic for you to make a profit from the niche you select:

- Motivation/Inspiration
- Success/Personal Development
- Business/Entrepreneurship
- Travel
- Lifestyle (ex. high-end luxury)
- Pets
- Finance
- Real Estate
- Religion
- Health
- Fitness/Nutrition
- Beauty

Every niche is going to have its advantages and disadvantages, so you need to choose the one that best suits you. Are you willing to put up with the disadvantages in your niche long enough to succeed and make money on Instagram even if it requires a lot of hard work? Even if you aren't planning to make money off of Instagram, choosing a niche with a huge audience is still key if you want to accelerate your growth and influence on Instagram.

I would like to remind you that I'm not putting these

criterias in this book to box you in a small hole. I'm doing this because changing your name later will have drastic consequences, especially if you have already acquired a respectable following. People will assume that a new person is managing the account and many of them will likely unfollow you.

Rather than go through this painful process of changing Instagram names, I highly recommend you pick a solid name that you will be proud to hold for the rest of your Instagram days. I cannot stress enough how important it is for you to choose a name that accurately represents you and your brand at the same time.

Remember that you can always use your overall page name (full name) to create the brand and then have your username come up more in the searches as people search for terms that are similar to your niche. People need to see your name and think about you, your brand and your business. Nothing more! That's how you get people talking about you and your brand.

In the next couple of chapters, you are going to learn how to model other successful pages to create your Instagram brand. Because it's far better to learn by standing on the shoulders of giants than trying to figure it all out by yourself. I've been there and it can be a very arduous process. Skip the unnecessary battles so that you can shorten your learning curve and accelerate your profits and growth on Instagram.

CHAPTER 3

Your Instagram Logo: Tiny Image, Massive Impact

The very first thing someone will notice when they visit your Instagram page will not be your content, it will be your logo. Your logo is your profile picture that represents you and your brand. You have one chance and one chance only to impress the person who is visiting your Instagram page with your logo. It's not enough to entice people with highly visual images on your profile, you must create a visual connection and that begins with your logo.

One of the main principles that you were taught about Instagram is that you have to be mobile-minded. What exactly does that mean? It means that people are not going to see an enlarged photo of your logo unless they go directly to your page. In fact, it will appear much smaller when people are scrolling through their newsfeeds and see it. In that tiny visual space, you need to capture someone's attention in less than a second.

Once you begin building an audience and engaging with your followers, your logo becomes an integral part of your brand's identity. For example, when your post comes up on your followers newsfeed, a powerful logo can catch their attention and if it's recognizable it might make the difference between the user stopping and engaging with your Instagram post or them simply scrolling right past it.

Also when you begin commenting on other people's posts, replying to comments on your own post or simply liking other people's comments, your logo will come up as a notification on the Instagram user's account. These small touchpoints that your brand has with these users is key to engaging with other accounts and your followers. A powerful logo that stands out in their notification or news feed is vital to grabbing their attention and placing your brand in the forefront of their mind on a consistent basis.

Here's two simple steps you can take to create an impactful logo for your Instagram page:

BE BOLD

Your logo has to stand out! It will be featured on the upper left-hand corner of every post that you make. One of the ways that you can do this is to use a white or dark background, and then have the logo pop out in contrast using an opposing color scheme.

Ultimately, your brand is going to be built and recognized based on your name, your logo and your content.

Your logo needs to catch the attention of other people if you are going to have your brand name recognized. When people visit your page for the first time you want to have a logo that is clear and concise in design. This could mean the difference between someone leaving your page immediately or becoming a loyal follower.

You know how people talk about Apple? When you see an Apple store, you don't even need to see the name "Apple". All it takes is a quick recognition of their trademark symbol and you immediately know who it is. You also know exactly what they do.

That's the type of instant recognition you want to achieve with your logo. You want your name and content spreading outside of the Instagram platform. People should look at your logo and recognize you and your brand in an instant.

BE SIMPLE

I love the quote that says: "The ultimate form of sophistication is simplicity. Perfection is not when nothing else can be added, but when nothing else can be taken away." Look at the largest and most influential Instagram pages, both overall and in your niche. You will notice that their logo is NOT complex – instead it's simple and to the point. There is no need for you to get fancy or worry about the intricate details. Instagram users are not going to be able to see tiny little details on their mobile phone and if it's too complex – they will have a hard time associating your logo with your brand.

When you see Nike's checkmark symbol, you don't have to think about what it is. You know exactly what it means and you know it the moment you see it. You don't want people to 'think' about your logo and what it represents.

BONUS: If you get really good, people will recognize you by a nickname. For example, Coca-Cola is commonly referred to as Coke. There's a popular page in my niche by the name of @AchieveTheImpossible. Their logo is a simple "ATI" – a typeface logo over a dark background. You want to know what everyone calls them? ATI. That's when you know that you got it right.

In fact, you will see a lot of businesses on Instagram using a simple typeface logo over a contrasting background. It looks super simple but it works every time. If you are stuck with ideas, it can't hurt to try a time-tested and simple strategy.

The Instagram page you create will partially dictate how you should approach designing your logo. As you read through the following descriptions that pertain to your page, keep in mind that the principles of being bold and simple still apply.

Business: You want a logo that represents your business. Nothing complex – just keep it simple. If your current logo is already complex, you want to opt for a simpler logo design that is not too far from your original logo. You don't want to change everything. Instagram is merely an extension of your existing core brand. Focus on what you already have, and simplify your logo for your Instagram page if it is currently too complex.

Personal: Go for a fun, professional picture that truly captures your real personality. You will probably have to take a few shots before you get it right, so take your time with it.

Niche Page: Make sure that your logo is as closely related to your brand as possible. Here, you will have to place a greater emphasis on making your logo bold. You really need to stand out if you want it to be recognizable to your brand exclusively.

Spend some time designing your logo but don't agonize over it for weeks on end. If you don't like the way your logo looks at first, you can always change it while you are still small in size. If you try to change it once you have a larger following, you will lose out on potential followers because now you no longer have a recognizable logo. You might have to essentially start from scratch again.

If you are struggling to come up with a logo that meets the criteria I discussed above, you can outsource the creation of your logo to a graphic designer. Websites like Fiverr, UpWork and 99Designs are great resources to connect with someone that can create a logo for you that represents you and your brand.

The best part is that you won't have to break the bank! You can get professional logos done anywhere from $5 all the way up to $1,000. Personally, I like 99Designs. com best and I believe you can get a great logo done for your brand page or company for about $50. If you are looking to keep your costs low for a logo specific for Instagram, simply ask the designer, on any of these websites, for a simple and bold type-based logo.

Remember, you don't have to be fancy, simple and clean will do the trick.

CHAPTER 4

How To Build A Bio/Profile That Generates BUYERS

After people see your eye-catching logo and your relevant username, they are going to take a quick peek at your bio/profile. Your profile is the text found on your Instagram page located directly below your logo. Now you don't have a lot of time here to make a good impression, you only have a few lines and that is it. Long form sales copy has no place in your bio/profile and it will repel more followers than it will attract.

There is a systematic way by which I chose to set up my bio/profile. You can use my template as a general guideline and try out different versions of your Instagram profile until you get it right. One of the great things about Instagram is how rapidly you can test ideas and get feedback on whether they are working or not.

Let's cover a few things that are integral to your Instagram bio/profile:

Bullet Points: You want your profile to feature bullet points and your phrases should occupy a single line. Your bio needs to be easy to read and right to the point. Play around with bullet points to get the ones that look clean and professional.

Concise: Since you are only focused on one line at a time, you have no choice but to keep things super simple. This makes your job a lot easier and people will be able to read your Instagram profile with ease. This way, there is no confusion whatsoever regarding your Instagram page and why it exists.

In summation, your bio/profile on Instagram should be clean and organized with content that people can absorb easily and quickly.

Right beneath your logo will be your profile name, which is separate from your actual page name. You can simply choose to re-state your page name unless you have something specific that you are focused on (ex. "Helping Entrepreneurs Succeed").

On the line below that, you can have a marketing message if it is consistently used across your marketing. For example, if I was Nike, I could put "Just Do It" in this line.

Once your profile name and tagline are intact, you're ready to move on to the core of your Instagram profile. Each and every line here counts, so pay close attention!

Your first line needs to be about your WHY – why did you create your brand. You want to generate curiosity and interest for the potential followers that are visiting your page. For example, @ElevateYourMindset has "Empowerment for Elevated Mindsets." This speaks directly to who I want to attract as my core follower base. It also creates a sense of community because the potential follower might feel included if they believe they have an elevated mindset. This is vital and you want to find something about your brand's 'why' that people can relate to and feel apart of.

Next, you want to focus on your WHAT. What is it that you are doing? What is it that you want people to do? If you are promoting a product, you should be direct and upfront about it. "Check out my latest confidence course" is direct and you are generating curiosity about this course in a simple way. Your Instagram profile is a great place to drive people to the link where your product is located (if it already has a website set up for it). You can easily MONETIZE your product or service this way!

I've personally found that if you have a finger emoji pointing down to your link, it serves as a strong and visual call to action for your followers to click the link and learn more about your products and services. You need to put a lot of thought into how you structure your bio if you want to drive traffic to your website or sales funnel.

Finally, the way you post the link in your bio/profile is crucial. People need to see your link and know that they are getting exactly what is advertised in your bio. If you have a product about confidence, the word 'confidence' should appear somewhere in the URL of your link. This means that if you are using a link shortening service like Bit.ly you need to put your product name in that URL. DO NOT put something like: bit.ly/2lrKZn5b. People will think it's a scam and they will not click on it. The link should look like: Bit.ly/Self-Confidence-Tips

Also, if you can, leave the "www" out and capitalize the first letter of the word in the name of your link "NameOfWebsite.com." I've found that I've got the highest number of clicks when links were simplified and spelled out with the first letter capitalized this way.

You generate curiosity, you establish your purpose, you guide them to your link through your call to action so they can learn more about that intriguing thing in your bio. If your sales funnel is setup properly, it will handle the rest. (In Chapter 21 we'll talk a lot more about setting up your sales funnel correctly). You can use your link to generate leads, build your email list, and make money!

Above all, your profile/bio has to reward the people who take the time to visit it and click on the link. The old school days of baiting people are over. As Gary Vaynerchuk says, you have to offer MASSIVE VALUE instead.

Here are a few more common tips that you should follow when creating your profile/bio:

4-LINE MAXIMUM

Unless you absolutely have to, keep your bio to four lines or less. And always make sure the product in the link is consistent with your shoutouts and promotions.

If you have a link in your bio, it MUST match up with the website link of the product or service that you are promoting. Promoting a video course only to drive people to an ebook will kill your traffic stream. People already know what they want before they visit your website and shattering that expectation will hurt your brand and drastically reduce your conversions.

Moreover, your profile/bio has to be consistent with

your promotion. Congruency in this Instagram-style sales funnel is key! People do not have the time or the attention span to try and figure out what you are promoting and they will simply move on to the next page if you lack congruence.

The design in the promotion and your website or sales funnel needs to match.

Once you have your ad/shoutout ready, you need to make sure that the design in your promotion AND marketing message are consistent. The messaging (i.e. your copy) and the color scheme need to match. I have seen my best conversion rates when I've kept these two things consistent in the promotion, bio AND website/sales funnel.

This means that your website or sales funnel, if that's your marketing vessel, needs to be highly visual (you'll learn a lot more about this throughout this book). People are accustomed to high-quality design and are extremely turned off by poor visuals, especially coming directly from Instagram which is filled with highly visual content. A lack of clean and crisp visuals will lead to low conversions. If your objective on Instagram is to get people to opt-in to your landing page or buy your products and services you will be extremely disappointed in your results if you design your webpages with low quality and/or pixelated images.

PUT YOUR CONTACT INFO ON THE BOTTOM OF YOUR PROFILE/BIO

Giving your followers a method to contact you directly is a great way to build long-term relationships and MAKE SALES. If you want to be contacted by email, list your email. If you want to be contacted by DM tell your followers that. Many Instagram Influencers like to communicate through the free app KIK, so that may be an option for you as well. Just make it abundantly clear how people who visit your Instagram page can contact you.

HAVE A STATEMENT THAT GIVES CREDIT TO PHOTOGRAPHERS

Some Instagram accounts, depending on the niche (ex. Continual reposts) might be subject to copyright infringement. If you will be reposting other people's Instagram content I highly recommend you put a "credits to all owners or photographers" statement at the top of your profile/bio. This will help safeguard your page from getting banned by Instagram.

Understand that your overall focus is to build a simple and clean bio/profile that's easy to read quickly. To achieve this you may need to use separators to give your page a neat and professional look. Signifiers like "|" can keep multiple pieces of information separate on a single line.

Even though you have a structured and well organized profile/bio, your goal is not to make it look pretty. The goal is to have a minimalist setup that is designed to achieve the singular purpose of monetization through the product or service that is accessible through the posted link in your bio. Nothing less, nothing more.

CHAPTER 5

Instagram Page Hacking:
How To Ethically Spy On & "Steal"
What the BIG Pages Are Doing

Tony Robbins, a world-renowned personal development guru, is well known for popularizing the concept of modelling. Tony says that when you want to achieve the same levels of success that other people have all you have to do is model their mindset and actions. This applies in many areas of life and monetary success on Instagram is no exception.

When I started building out my Instagram page, I didn't just look at successful pages in my niche, I studied them. I looked to see if there were any similarities in how they were designing their name, their logo and their bio.

I asked myself: What were these massive Instagram

pages doing? What were they not doing? How were they doing it?

You need to become insanely curious about what these big Instagram pages are doing if you want to have a following like they do in the near future. You also want to avoid modeling yourself after pages that are unsuccessful for obvious reasons.

Later on, you will receive an invaluable tool that tells you if a page is ACTUALLY successful. It is easy to be deceived into thinking that a page is successful on the surface until you dig deep and look at the hard data. You will also learn how this modelling process applies to creating your own successful sales funnel.

In my case, I was looking at the personal development and motivation niche. ThinkGrowProsper, AchieveTheImpossible, Motivated.Mindset and Millionaire_ Mentor are four stand-out pages that I chose to model my Instagram page after (ElevateYourMindset).

Here are some specific things that I found when I was examining these large Instagram pages:

CONTENT

These pages CONSISTENTLY delivered amazing content on a regular basis (sometimes up to 14 posts per day). This is a huge part of why they were able to build such a strong brand and stay in the forefront of people's minds on an ongoing basis.

NAME

Their name shows a benefit – when you read them, it is clear that you get some type of benefit or result from following them. Their names are also recognizable and they stand out in a niche where pages are constantly created on a daily basis. You want to follow them right away because you already know that they are going to add value to your life (ex. Millionaire_Mentor mentors you to become a millionaire, Motivated.Mindset motivates you to think abundantly, and Achieve The Impossible helps you...well, I'll leave that one up to you to figure out).

LOGO

The designs used in their logo influenced how I designed my logo along with the advice that you received two chapters ago. The typebased logos were clean and they really pop out immediately at first glance. They each used a simple background and used logos that contrasts sharply in color. This allows them to really stand out when people are scrolling through their newsfeeds. ThinkGrowProsper did something unique – they put an open book at the bottom half of their logo to build a strong brand that conveys to people that an open book is as powerful as an open mind. Simple, yet effective!

PROFILE/BIO

Each of these massive pages had a short yet strong message with very clear bullet points that directed you to the link in their bio via a call to action. ThinkGrowProsper often uses the word "FREE" in their bio/profile. You will later learn how powerful this word can be when you're trying to increase traffic to your website or sales funnel.

Many of these Instagram brands are so powerful that dozens if not hundreds of people have gone so far as to copy their logos, names and bios. Don't be a copycat! Use their overall profile as a blueprint for your own brand. Being original is the only way to build your own unique and recognizable brand.

HOMEWORK: Do some research and create a list of pages in your niche that you want to model. Once you have this list ready, you will want to sift through them and see which ones are legitimately growing and which ones are fake. You will learn how to do this in chapter 10.

@ tezzamb

@ gypsea-lust and @ doyoutravel

@ deanastasia

@ vanellimelli

@

CHAPTER 6

How To Select The Perfect Niche & Deliver Content That Turns Your Followers Into Raving Fans & Paying Customers

You have to continuously remind yourself that Instagram is first and foremost a mobile platform. What does this mean? Everything needs to be tailored and optimized for people to easily and quickly digest on their phones. That includes the psychological tactics that you use to get people to stop scrolling and engage with your post.

Nothing will contribute to your organic growth more than the content that you post. For this reason, you need to target a niche that is 'just right'. You don't want to be so narrow that a small number of people take interest, but not so broad that your purpose is unclear to a person who is seeing your page for the first time. With this being the case, your passion might not necessarily be the best thing to create an Instagram page about. This is especially true if your goal is to turn Instagram into a monetization platform.

Here's how things work in the online world: On a website, you usually have 3 to 5 seconds to make a good first impression before the user decides if they want to stay on your page or click the red "X" button. It is nothing BUT the first impression that counts. With an Instagram photo, you have 1 second at best to make that impression.

Think about how your average Instagram user browses through their newsfeed: Many Instagram users have hundreds of people they are following. They don't have time to individually process hundreds of images. They will scroll through them at break-neck speeds until they find something that catches their eye or is relatable to them. You could even say that it's quite the thumb workout!

Your marketing on Instagram needs to be super simple and crystal clear. You cannot afford anything else in the one small opportunity you get to draw the user into the desired action (visit your website, comment on your photo, etc.). Therefore, your content strategy needs to be the same way.

The old business adage of providing high quality content does not change when it comes to building your Instagram page. For thousands of years, people always followed those who provide nothing but value and your overall strategy on Instagram should not ignore this vital truth.

As you build your loyal community of followers you

will learn exactly what they want, how to give it to them and when to give it to them. You will not have to sit there scratching your head because the numbers will speak for themselves. The fact that you can track so many vital metrics on Instagram is what allows you to see the results of your changes in real-time. A/B testing has never been simpler.

There is a lot to digest in this chapter, but it's vitally important that you develop a value-packed content strategy that is based on proven methods. This will be your foundation for all of your content creation as you begin to grow your Instagram following. It will also guide you as you continue to create content far into the future. So get ready to take some notes!

TIPS

Here are some tips that you can follow to ensure you are providing your user base with the best Instagram content they can find in your niche. This applies to the posts that you share and the captions within them.

YOU NEED TO BE SPECIFIC

With the size of Instagram's platform, you cannot be everything to everyone. It simply won't work. You will be spreading yourself too thin and taking yourself away from the value that you could be providing to a niche community of your choice. Almost every industry has jumped on the Instagram train to build up enormous audiences through sheer hard work and dedication. It did not happen overnight nor by accident.

Whether you are a business or a brand, you need to

decide what you are going to be and who you are going to target. This is the key to consistently providing your followers with high-quality content that adds value to their life.

You need to spend time researching your community and their needs. Look at your competitors – the top performers in your niche and see the content they are posting. See the trends that are hot right now. Look at the people following them and the other kinds of pages that they are following.

However, don't miss the forest for the trees. You need to see what the audience at large is looking at and not just a few followers. You want to post content that people will INTERACT with. That means content that they will comment on, like, and share with their friends and followers.

You need to develop content that is catered to your niche market and the broader range of people who are interested in the same category. After all, you are looking for a wide range of followers. This will require that you research different sub-niches to identify audiences that might also be interested in your content.

You have the opportunity right now to demonstrate your knowledge as an authority in your niche and connect with people at a deep level. Think about your ideal audience and the content that best resonates with them. What gets the most engagement? What doesn't? You want to know what to post, but you also want to know what you shouldn't post.

Do not overwhelm your followers with ads.

We will talk more about this in a later chapter, but you

will be able to leverage your platform for promotions/ shoutouts and other opportunities that will provide you with a substantial source of income. However, the biggest mistake people make here is that they turn their Instagram page into an advertisement billboard. Understand: People do not watch TV for the commercials.

Your followers are real people! They want content and FREE VALUE before you try and sell them something.

Your followers are smarter than you may think. The moment you begin flooding your Instagram page with ads they will see through your actions and know that you have effectively 'sold out'. What was once an Instagram page filled with value has now become a billboard for other people to sell their products and gain exposure. That's a huge turn off to the majority of your follower base regardless of the niche you select.

I would personally recommend that you only promote products and services on your own page no more than a few times a week, and only leaving the promotion/shoutouts up for no longer than 6 hours at a time. This is not a hard and fast rule but from experience it strikes the right balance along with delivering the best results.

This is different for each niche. But experiment with frequency and duration of promotion posting to see what will work best for you. Remember that you can always track your engagement and other metrics to see how things are working out (In chapter 8 I am going to show you the software I use to track my engagement on Instagram).

If you are going to be posting advertisements for other pages and other people's products, keep it at 90% value content and only 10% ads. By posting ads less frequently, people will actually see them and get the impression that they can add value to your page and their life. (Later in this book we'll talk about where you should be posting your Instagram ads on a daily basis.)

YOU NEED TO BE CONSISTENT

Your followers are going to be on Instagram every day and they expect you to deliver on a regular basis. When they know that you are going to be posting valuable content multiple times a day, they will continue to follow you. They can't wait until you deliver that next piece of content that improves their lives and helps them learn something new. They look to you for guidance, advice and the next best thing and you need to be there to provide it for them. If not, somebody else is going to take your place along with the money you could be earning.

If you fall off and don't post for a few days, your engagement rate will drop exponentially and you will be cast into the Instagram page graveyard.

People will forget about you very quickly and your brand won't be associated with a lot of value. Once that happens it takes TEN TIMES more work to climb up that hill and get back to where you previously were. So be sure to stay consistent.

My page (ElevateYourMindset) consistently delivers value at least 2 or 3 times a day. I rarely go a day without posting at least twice and not a single day goes by where I don't post at all. Active engagement and posting regularly is the key to building a steadily growing follower base but most importantly, it helps you build a community of raving fans.

You want people to engage with your brand and your posts on a daily basis. The more you post (not too much – more on that later), the more your followers will love you. They will like your posts and comment on them. That can translate into new leads, customers, clients or whatever it is you are looking to achieve on Instagram.

SHARE USEFUL CONTENT FROM OTHER INSTAGRAM PAGES

Occasionally you will find that other Instagram pages deliver a message that you aren't able to. If you feel that it will add value to your community, you can share useful content and expose your followers to new insights. A motivational video, an unheard of yet useful quote – it could be anything. If you choose to share content, make sure you credit the person who originally posted it. You don't want to get into a fight about stealing content. This is something that you should use sparingly as you are directing people to other Instagram pages.

VISUALS, VISUALS, VISUALS

Remember that Instagram is a highly visual platform. Therefore, you need to be using high-quality photos in every post that you make. They need to be crisp, high definition, and high resolution. Using pixelated images is unacceptable.

When you use high-quality images, people see that your brand is a REAL brand. This is especially vital if you are aiming to be a high-end luxury brand. Take a look at the high-end pages on Instagram – you won't find a single photo that is anything less than stellar in quality and definition.

FOCUS ON WHAT WORKS BEST FOR YOUR NICHE

For your specific market, you need to model huge pages with high rates of engagement and focus only on what works. This will require you to go deep into analytics and find the best pages to model. In later chapters I will cover exactly how this can be done. Modeling large Instagram pages is the fastest way to figure out what content is worth emulating and sharing.

Once you figure out what works, stick to it! You want to avoid posts that differ from what is tried and true. How do you know what works? You want to focus on the posts that keep you at an engagement rate of 2% or better (we'll talk more about engagement rates in the next chapter).

Remember what you learned earlier in this book about emulating successful Instagram pages: You want to model their content, but you do not want to copy it!

USE VARIETY TO ATTRACT NEW FOLLOWERS

A common mistake amongst new Instagram users is to post the same type of content every day: The exact background color on each post, the same type of text, the exact same design. When you do this, your followers quickly get bored and they may even unfollow you.

Although you do want to stick with what works, you also want to introduce variety into your posts. In doing so, you are taking a step or two outside your target market to attract followers that could potentially be interested in your content. You want to use different styles of posts that resonate with different types of followers.

With enough variety in your posting, there is bound

to be certain things that will resonate with an Instagram user and convert them into one of your loyal followers.

I've personally tested posting the same type of images throughout an entire week and I noticed that my engagement took a sharp drop! I've even seen that the most successful pages that I modeled my page after are constantly using variety in their posts.

So, how do you stay consistent yet use variety with your content? This is something where testing is your best friend. I couldn't possibly tell you what will be best for your page without knowing your niche and your brand.

Test EVERYTHING. Try backgrounds of different colors. Alternate between a person in the image and a plain background. Use different types of texts and fonts. See which backgrounds and styles resonate most with your audience. Given how rapidly things move on Instagram, you will be able to A/B test multiple options in a short amount of time. It should take you no longer than a few days to see what works and what doesn't.

Here's what you'll end up with: You will have a few styles and backgrounds that resonate most with people. Backgrounds of certain color might give you the best engagement rates. Certain fonts might do the same thing. Perhaps different styles of posts (self-depreciating humor, inspirational quotes, actionable advice, info graphics, etc.) will resonate best with your followers.

Personally, I have five different styles that I consistently use day in and day out. That is more than enough – you could even shorten that down to 3 or 4. The key is to leverage variety so that you can cater to your follower's needs while attracting new followers.

Here's a quick pro tip for when you start building momentum and your follower base begins growing quickly – learn from your testing and find a consistent theme for your page. For example, when I hit around 75,000 followers I began to notice that other pages in my niche were posting similar content (successful men and women with motivational quotes) and I saw my engagement began decreasing percentage wise. So I studied all the successful pages in my niche and found two or three that were growing extremely fast and modeled them directly. They all had a consistent theme both visually and message wise.

Now my strategy involves a dark and white theme with very few images and mostly (98%) simple clean posts with black or gray backgrounds with white text or white backgrounds with dark gray text. I also use about 3 to 4 different font types to keep it consistent but also provide some variety.

Something else I did was take a close look at what pieces of content we're getting better engagement and narrowed in on a few key message points that appealed most to my audience. After I focused on delivering the kind of value my audience wanted, my engagement increased substantially.

So when you begin growing in the tens of thousands of followers I suggest you take a close look at your content and the other successful pages in your niche and develop a theme for your own page that is consistent but has elements of variety. In the beginning this isn't that important and you'll be testing and gathering data from your engagement rates so only focus heavily on this strategy once your page starts growing fast which can happen quickly once you begin implementing the strategies in this book.

COMMITMENT IS #1!

Even if it takes some time to discover what your followers want, keep posting content daily because your content will still provide value. It's not mindless posting because your post is there to give value to your current followers and soon-to-be followers.

As you deliver content on a daily basis, remember that it is FREE on Instagram to build your community. Stay the course and eventually you will get to the point where you start getting followers that will be converted into email subscribers, leads and money in your bank account.

You must be committed to building your Instagram page and stay consistent with publishing new content. It is still surprising to see how many people don't understand this basic fact.

Right now, there are a lot of pages in your market that are getting hundreds if not thousands of followers on a daily basis. If they can do it, so can you. It will take time, but all great things in life take time. Nobody become successful on Instagram overnight. Always remember: Anything in life that comes easy and fast will leave you the exact same way.

CHAPTER 7

How To Create A Steady Flow of High-Quality, Engaging Images In Under 5 Minutes A Day

Now that you know the importance of posting high-quality content on a regular basis and have a foundation for your content strategy, you need to know how to create it. What you probably don't know is that it doesn't have to be a laborious process. The truth is, it will only take you a couple of minutes to create a great post that you can share with your followers to add value to their lives and further engage with them.

The name of the game is EFFICIENT content creation. You don't want to spend more time than necessary to create content, especially when the content must be delivered as consistently as possible on Instagram. When you grow in size and you need to post more often throughout the day, you will have no choice but to be as efficient as possible.

There are three software programs that you can use to create high-quality content in only a few seconds. There are several tutorials online on how you can use these applications, but they are extremely easy to pick up and it only takes a few minutes to learn how to use them.

The first application is WordSwag, a free mobile app that you can download to your phone. You can take a high-resolution background image, overlay some custom text on top of it, and even add your watermark logo on your image as well. For your logo, make sure that it is a preloaded image with a transparent background. This allows your logo to fit on any image regardless of color. You can change its brightness in the software application if you want your logo to have a softer feel on your posts.

The next application is Adobe Post. Like WordSwag, it is free to download. This one is far more heavy in design and comes with several pre-loaded templates that you can add text to. There is a lot more flexibility but there is a steeper learning curve if you want to take full advantage of all of its functionality.

The last application is Phonto. This is my personal favorite. And if you sign up for my Instagram webclass: www.FreeIGTraining.com you will get instant access to a video tutorial where I walk you through step-by-step how to create eye-catching images with this app in only a few seconds.

Since you will be sharing high-quality images on a regular basis, I highly recommend you get the app Phonto.

You can take an image that you are about to post and adjust several features: Sharpness, temperature, lightness, saturation, and many more. You can play around with the settings until you get the re-adjusted image that looks good enough for you to post on your Instagram page.

There are other applications you can use that will provide similar results, and I will include those in the Appendix of this book. However, everything you need for high quality content creation is within the three apps I just mentioned.

NOTE: If you are a personal brand, you want to focus on keeping your photos very personal. Your personal life, your business life – everything should be centered around your daily activities. Garyvee is a great example of someone who manages to get his personal brand down and create massive influence.

I would also like to share some resources that I use to find royalty free photos. These are images that you can repurpose into content that you can share on your Instagram page. These resources are helpful for people who are in niches where it is difficult to get their own original photos without excessive labor (ex. Travel, luxury).

Pexels.com, Unsplash.com and FreeImages.com are three resources that provide you with high-quality royalty free pictures. You can download these pictures to your phone and touch them up using the apps I just talked about.

Here's a quick pro tip that will help you subtly brand your Instagram page – when using these apps to create posts you want to make sure you are using some type of logo to brand them effectively without "over-branding" to the point where people will think twice about sharing them. I like to use a simple type based logo within all of my images and to do this efficiently I use a simple font to spell out my Instagram page name when creating my posts. This allows me to keep my images super clean without over-branding them with a logo that may prevent people from sharing my content (ex. Taking a screenshot of my post and sharing it on Facebook).

When I started doing this I saw my content being shared at a much higher rate and it is so easy to implement that it almost feels like cheating. If you go with a similar strategy just make sure you are using only ONE font for this to ensure your design is consistent and people can begin associating your branded logo easily. Having too many fonts will dilute your brand and cause confusion. To get some inspiration you can visit my page and view how I use this font for branding my images with my type-based logo @ElevateYourMindset.

REPURPOSING/REUSING CONTENT

Let's do some simple math: Let's say you follow my recommendation and post 3 times a day. That's 270 posts over a 3-month period. I don't know about you, but that seems like a lot of content. Way too much, in fact. With the best pages on Instagram, you'll notice that most of them do not have hundreds upon thousands of posts. There are merely a few hundred or a few thousand that get repurposed (i.e. posted again) from time to time.

This is a huge relief for people who overwhelm themselves from the very beginning with all the work that has to be done. Don't get the wrong idea – there is a lot of hard work involved behind setting up a successful

Instagram page, but at the same time you don't want to make things harder than they have to be.

As your following begins to grow and you start posting images on your Instagram page, it will not take you very long to figure out what's working and what isn't working. You'll see the posts that your followers don't like in the form of low engagement through a lack of likes and comments. When you figure out what people like, that's when you can repurpose the content that gives you the best engagement.

After a period of about 6 to 8 weeks, you can browse through your old content and repurpose the posts that received the best engagement. I can tell you from personal experience that this strategy works great. Here's why: When you shared that content 6 to 8 weeks ago, that was with your followers at that particular point in time. Now, you have a huge group of new followers that haven't seen what you posted a month or a few months ago. Simply put, the majority of your community hasn't seen that content yet and they haven't had the opportunity to benefit from it or engage with it. It's almost like a new post made from scratch. Also chances are the original group of followers who liked or commented on that post initially won't recognize the fact you are reusing that image and most likely will like or comment on it again.

Even though I showed you how to efficiently create high-quality content, it doesn't take away from the fact that it still takes a lot of time at 20 plus posts per week. Reposting images or videos allows you to post content that engages with your followers at a high level since you are repurposing content that has been proven to generate likes and comments. This is a great way to work smart instead of hard.

It's a win-win situation for you and your followers. You focus on high-value content to ensure that your engagement rates steadily improve, AND you have fresh content for your new followers that you know will enjoy and interact with that particular post.

This will keep your followers focused and engaged with your Instagram posts on a consistent basis. You will see your engagement steadily increase with this strategy. It's fresh content for new and old followers and it's content you know they will all love.

You're now beginning to move towards a steady path of learning how you can monetize your Instagram page without having to post 3 to 5 times a day and spend hours designing images.

SHORT TERM SACRIFICES PRODUCE LONG TERM SUCCESS

Understand, when you are starting off, the process of gaining organic followers is extremely labor-intensive. It will take a lot of dedication and self-discipline before you can gradually slow down. Don't listen to the hype from successful Instagram Influencers who try to sell you on how relaxing and comfortable their lifestyles were when they were building their massive followings. Unless they bought an Instagram page (which I do not recommend anyone do) I guarantee you they put in an extraordinary amount of work and went through a ton of trial and error before they saw their efforts pay off.

In fact, your first 10,000 followers are going to be the most difficult to obtain. You will find that building your Instagram following cuts into other activities that are part of your daily schedule. Giving up on the notion of

balance is essential to creating a massive follo~
short amount of time. I told you in the introductior.
book that this was going to require hard work, b. ~ne
message is worth repeating.

All of the notifications and pings you will get on your
phone are going to drain your battery like nothing else. It
would be wise to keep your phone attached to a charger
at all times, or at least invest in a charging dock or a por-
table battery that you can use. This allows you to leave
your phone by your computer so that you can stay up to
date with activity on your Instagram page.

For many people, growing and monetizing an Instagram page begins as only a side hustle, but you must
take it serious from the onset. While you can work on
your Instagram page from anywhere in the world, the
beginning will be rough. Only in the future will you be
able to relax while managing and making money off your
Instagram page.

You might even have to cut your meals short and
reduce the amount of sleep you are accustomed to getting for a while so you can stay engaged with your followers. The more you can create a connection with your
community, the better your engagements rates will be.
Growing an Instagram following requires a major investment of your time, but fortunately, Instagram continues
to make it easier for us to engage with our followers: We
can now 'like' the comments they leave on our posts.

Personally, I spend a tremendous amount of time
replying to comments, answering direct messages and
liking the majority of comments I receive on my posts.
I do this (and you should too) because it allows me to
expand on the amount of touchpoints and interactions

I have with my followers. My favorite strategy is liking each of the comments I get on my posts, specifically because it requires practically no effort and the commenter will receive a notification that I liked their post thus creating another touchpoint or notification they can associate to me and my brand.

Ignore the people who sell you the dream of "effortless prosperity". Growing your following and making money on Instagram requires more than just posting and closing the app.

Your free time is now your Instagram time. Eventually, you'll reach the point where you only have to post for a few minutes a day, but right now you are probably not at that point. The only thing you can do is look forward and focus on what you are going to do in the moment and the near future. After 6 to 8 months of hard work and intense effort, you can look back and bask in all the incredible progress you have made. By then you will be able to relish in the self-satisfaction that you succeeded and proved the naysayers wrong (trust me...there will be naysayers and they will try to talk you out of succeeding regardless of what avenue you pursue in life).

Building a successful Instagram page that generates predictable profits is filled with setbacks and bumps in the road, especially when you're just starting out. There were several times I wanted to quit. But wanting to and actually doing it is what makes all the difference.

The success I currently have on Instagram was earned through sheer hard work and relentless persistence. I would not trade what I have right now for anything else in the world. And I want you to feel the exact same way after a year has passed from the moment that you read this book.

CHAPTER 8

How To Time Your Instagram Posts & Shoutouts for Maximum: Engagement, Followers & Buyers

You might not have realized it yet, but the time of day when you post on your own Instagram page as well as when you post shoutouts on Instagram Influencer's pages will make a big difference in your engagement and conversions.

Many of the big pages have international reputations. They have followers from all over the world which means that they have to take into account all of the different time zones. When you are setting up your shoutout schedule, you need to think worldwide. To be more specific, at the time I am writing this I have over 200,000 followers and 57% of them are international, so this point cannot be emphasised enough.

If you post a shoutout at the early morning hour of 3am US EST, your promotion will be seen by a certain group of people. Post that same shoutout 12 hours later, and you will have access to an entirely different group of people.

→ When you are setting up a schedule for posting your shoutouts, you should aim to post on 2 to 3 pages a day (make certain you are tracking each shoutout individually), each at a different time. Not only do you allow the majority of people on other pages to see your posts, but when they see it enough times on separate pages they will be more enticed to visit your website. If your sales copy is compelling enough and you have a solid product, you'll have a buyer!

If you are posting advertisements on your own page, you can place them in-between your regular content but be sure to remove them after about 6 hours. Remember the rule from the previous chapter – the vast majority of time you need to be posting value-based content that is in the form of high quality images and possibly videos.

As for posting personal content on your own page, you will eventually create a content schedule that works best for you and your page. People will know what to expect and when to expect it. The more you meet that expectation, the more loyal your followers will be and the more you will attract new followers. This is how you build trust and integrity with the community you are building on Instagram. You don't ever want to leave your followers hanging!

You also want to be consistent not only in how frequently you post but also in the volume that you are posting. If you are posting several bulk images at once, you are harming your Instagram brand in several ways.

For one, you will receive lower engagement on each individual post because it's too much for your followers to go through. Second, you are giving off the impression of a spam page that is not run by a real person. Third, you might come across as an advertisement heavy page which will turn your followers off. People aren't naïve in the online world and they will quickly catch on to this and unfollow you.

The best way to go about it is to post 2 to 4 times a day, with the posts being spaced out evenly. Posts should be at least 4 hours apart. I have noticed that publishing two photos at the same time, advertisement or original content, leads to lower engagement and a lower number of followers gained, if any. You will have to experiment with the time of day you post to see when the best times are for you to gain new followers and get the best engagement on your images.

The right balance will have people excited to receive high-quality content from you without believing that you are spamming them or overwhelming them. If you post too much, you are getting in the way of posts that they want to see from their friends and other pages that they follow on their personal newsfeed. Excess posting is a great way to encourage your followers to click the 'Unfollow' button! All of this is entirely dependent on your niche and type of followers you attract. Even then, you will have to do some individual testing to figure this out for yourself.

Once your page becomes larger, you can slowly but carefully experiment with posting more often. You can post more original content and advertisements/ shoutouts.

ICONOSQUARE

What I want to encourage you to do is use a tool like Iconosquare to determine the best times of the day to post for your target demographic. You will be able to see how engaged your audience is and specifically when that engagement is occurring. The app records your posting times and shows your audience engagement over a 24-hour period. You can see which days are important and which times of the day are best for posting. If you have your Facebook page attached to your Instagram page you will get analytics directly from your Instagram page, but I still like to use Iconosquare.

You need to use analytical tools to get the best information since you will not be able to deduce this by simply looking at your individual pieces of content on your Instagram page. Once you have this setup you can create a pipeline where posts are delivered at a preset schedule. You won't be able to do this automatically since Instagram's API does not allow third party apps to post content in your place. (Note: There are third party apps that do this but they violate Instagram's Terms of Service and are likely to get your account banned so proceed with extreme caution if you are looking into this type of automation.)

INFOGRAPHICS

Don't bother wasting your time with infographics that tell you the best times of the day and the days when you should be posting. There are too many variables to take into account that will completely change what works best for each Instagram page.

So start posting, testing and tracking and soon enough you will know the ideal times to post on your own page to increase engagement as well as the optimal times to post shoutouts to increase your traffic to your sales funnel and ultimately generate predictable profits from your Instagram page.

CHAPTER 9

Instagram Identity Theft: Why Getting Ripped Off Means You're On the Right Track

Although you probably won't have to worry about Instagram's verification until you begin to have people copying your page, it is something that deserves a brief chapter of its own.

If you are a frequent user of Facebook, YouTube or Twitter, you will notice that certain profiles have started receiving a blue badge next to their name. The purpose of this badge is to provide an official sign to users that the person behind the profile is who they say they are.

On the Instagram platform, they are currently hand-picking users to give this coveted badge too. From what I've seen, the users who have several impersonator accounts are the ones that are getting first dibs. These fake accounts do a significant amount of damage to the Instagram pages they are copying and/or pretending to be. They delude followers into following the wrong person and they degrade the connections these profiles have with people that already have verified pages. Chances are, if there are a large number of false accounts for an Instagram page, they probably have a decent amount of power and influence.

It's important to know that the blue badge next to an Instagram user's name is regarded as a major status symbol on Instagram.

When Instagram verifies your account it will do wonders to boost the networking opportunities that you can obtain through Instagram. Depending on your niche, you can leverage them and obtain some serious benefits. Your customer base is also boosted because now you have a sign of legitimacy that few others have. Many Instagram Influencers double, or even triple their fees to post promotions once their account gets verified by Instagram.

WARNING: DO NOT try to create your own fake accounts in hopes of getting your account verified by Instagram. This is against the terms of use and your account will likely be suspended or banned.

CHAPTER 10

Shoutouts & Instagram Influencers: How To Get Famous Instagrammers To Promote Your Page & Products

For the vast majority of people, businesses and brands who begin using Instagram, the initial objective is to get followers so they can build a community of raving fans who will want to purchase their products and services. In order to build your community you must first learn how to increase your brand's exposure by getting more people to visit your Instagram page. The more people who visit your page the more followers you will obtain therefore increasing the influence of yourself and your brand which will allow you to create an asset that you can leverage to deliver value, market your products or services and ultimately grow your business and generate predictable profits.

The most powerful marketing strategy you can utilize

on Instagram to increase your page's exposure consists of leveraging the power of 'Instagram Influencers'. When done correctly, this can grow your Instagram following fast along with drive tons of warm leads to your website or sales funnel on a consistent basis. This is the exact strategy I used to not only build a community of well over 100,000 followers in less than six months but also to create an automated flow of steady traffic into my sales funnels.

The process by which you can leverage an Instagram Influencer's community to promote your page, product or service all begins with what is called a 'shoutout'. A shoutout involves sharing a post to feature another page or product ("go follow this person" or "go buy this product").

Since the beginning of Instagram, this is one of the most basic ways through which you can increase your following and sell your products and services on Instagram without needing to go through Facebook's confusing ad platform. You simply connect with an Instagram Influencer, pay them to post a screenshot of your page or share a post with your product in it along with a personal endorsement that encourages people to follow your page or buy your product or service.

The concept of 'influencer marketing' did not originate on Instagram, it is widely used through almost every type of media where marketers spend their time. Yet to this day using Instagram Influencers to build a community and drive traffic remains an overlooked and drastically misunderstood strategy by the vast majority of marketers. Their lack of awareness of the raw power of Instagram only makes it easier for people like you to take advantage of this amazing opportunity and begin using Instagram as an asset to launch and grow your business faster than ever before.

Leveraging Instagram Influencers is very simple in nature but to understand the fundamentals along with the specific time-tested techniques we are going to need to dive deep into the overall strategy one step at a time. Whether you are looking to grow your follower base, drive traffic to your website or sales funnel or accomplish both of these objectives simultaneously, there are multiple free and paid strategies that you can begin utilizing today. So let's break them down beginning with the free strategies for growing your follower base.

SHOUTOUT-FOR-SHOUTOUT (S4S)

One of the most common ways people build their communities on Instagram is by using a shoutout-for-shoutout or what some people refer to as a share-for-share (S4S). The way this works is you find a page with a similar follower base (in terms of niche and follower count) and you shoutout each others Instagram page. You are essentially partnering with another Instagram page with the objective of tapping into their community to increase your brand's exposure and attract new followers.

The process by which you introduce your brand to your shoutout partner's community is simple and incredibly easy to execute. You create a piece of branded and value based content that the person's audience/followers you are partnering with would benefit from. Beyond the highly visual image you want to create a compelling caption that entices their followers to visit your page and follow you. Make sure your Instagram username is in the first line of the caption to make it easy to view without having the user expand the caption in order to see your Instagram name. Many times I like to put a space in the caption after I have already inserted my Instagram name and then put it three more times in a row just to make it extremely easy for people to click it and follow my page.

When you are forming partnerships with people on Instagram for the purpose of doing a shoutout-for-shoutout the key component that drives this relationship is 'an equal exchange of value'. You want to make sure that when you are establishing a shoutout partnership both you and the person you are going to be shouting out are benefitting equally. If someone has half your follower base, they need to do 2 shoutouts for each one you post for them. So for example, if you have 3,000 followers and someone with 1,500 followers reaches out to you for a shoutout partnership, they would need to do 2 shoutouts in exchange for you giving them one shoutout.

When I was initially trying to grow my Instagram following I routinely reached out to pages that had 3 times the amount of followers I had and offered to shout their page out 3 times in exchange for them shouting my page out once. It was a great strategy that really helped me grow my following fast. I highly recommend you reach out to pages that have 3 times more followers than you and work out a partnership that will allow you both to grow your follower base quickly.

When you have the right partnerships, shout-out-for-shoutouts can be an extremely effective way to increase the exposure of your page and increase your follower base quickly. That being said, there is a way to expand your reach without increasing your efforts. This can be done through shoutout groups.

SHOUTOUT GROUPS

Shoutouts groups, or what is also referred to as 'shoutout trains' leverage the power of a group of Instagram pages to multiply the exposure for everyone involved. Essentially, a group of active users will get together and start a 'train' where an individual gives a shoutout to one of the members in the group, followed by the second person shouting out the first person, followed by the third person shouting out the second person, and so on. All of this happens within a short period of time and it takes advantage of the snowball effect, where you are tapping into a ton of Instagram users.

You will notice that as you grow your following and work with Instagram users who have larger follower bases, the effect continues to compound. You tap into a larger base of Instagram users, which means more followers for your page. In turn, once your Instagram account begins to grow in size, you become a more attractive prospect and people will invite you to join their shoutout groups. It's a self-fulfilling cycle that benefits you as you continue to grow your Instagram following.

Shoutout partnerships and shoutout groups can be a great way to grow your Instagram page, but they can also be harmful to your long-term growth if they are used carelessly or too frequently. Remember your followers chose to follow you for YOUR content, not other people's.

A WARNING ABOUT SHOUTOUT-FOR-SHOUTOUT (S4S)

You may be tempted to do a shoutout-for-shoutout with someone who has a larger follower base than you but has content that will not add value to your followers. If you choose to accept shoutout partners like this, you will hurt your brand and possibly lose the followers you worked hard to attract. On the other hand, the content you create for your shoutout partner's page should add value to their followers as well. Just remember, always deliver value and always keep your community in mind before you set up a new partnership.

Branding is E-V-E-R-Y-T-H-I-N-G on Instagram so proceed with caution before you partner with anyone on Instagram with the objective of trading shoutouts.

If you take a look at my Instagram page (ElevateYour-Mindset), you will see that I stay true to this principle. Shoutouts are rarely (if ever) done because it's time and space where my followers don't get to connect with the content that I tailored to meet their needs. My golden rule for shoutout-for-shoutout partnerships is simple – always guard your brand's reputation with your life.

Although the above strategies are effective when used properly and cost little or nothing to utilize, they are not the fastest way to grow your follower base. The core strategy for growing your follower base extremely fast is simple – you pay Instagram Influencers to promote your Instagram page.

PURCHASING SHOUTOUTS FOR FOLLOWERS

Now this differs from the techniques previously mentioned because this will require an actual investment. You are essentially purchasing a shoutout from a page within your niche that is much larger than yours. Simply put, you are buying time on an Instagram Influencer's newsfeed and therefore increasing the exposure for your page. If you provide great content on your page (as outlined in chapter 7) more people will be compelled to follow you because they see value.

This strategy is by far one of the best if you are looking to grow your follower base quickly simply because you can focus on purchasing shoutouts from pages that are much larger than yours and you don't have to worry about an equal value exchange in terms of their follower base since you are paying for the shoutout. This will also protect your own brand since you have no obligation to share another Instagram users content.

Here are six ways people are using Instagram Influencers to grow their Instagram following:

1. The Instagram Influencer takes a screenshot of your page and features your last 9 images on their page and in the caption tells people to follow you.

2. The Instagram Influencer takes one of your original posts, copies it or redesigns it and features it on their page and tells their followers to follow you.

3. The Instagram Influencer creates their usual branded content but gives you a shoutout in the caption.

4.   The Instagram Influencer posts your Instagram name on their story feature and tells people to follow you.

5.   The Instagram Influencer does a live video telling people to follow you and pins your Instagram name on a comment while they are doing the live video.

6.   The Instagram Influencer does a video telling people to follow you and posts it to their story.

From my experience #1 and #6 gets you the most followers while #2 and #3 provide decent results. For the record #5 generates the least followers.

Ninja Hack: After an extraordinary amount of testing shoutouts I have found that when you post four images on a single post (collage) and then write above the image: "Follow My NEW Favorite Instagram Page" that generates the best results. The reason why is because when you just share a normal post many of the pages' followers do not realize it's a shoutout therefore they do not engage with the post and in turn they do not go follow you.

When you use the paid shoutout strategy, make sure you choose an Instagram Influencer that has a substantial following. Anyone who has less than 100,000 followers is not going to send many people to your page. I suggest when you are getting started with paid shoutouts you look for Instagram pages that have 100k to 200K followers so you can test the engagement and the amount of followers you get.

You can expect to pay anywhere from $20 (100k to 300K) to $300 (1M and up) for a paid shoutout and obviously the bigger the page the more followers you will attract. Understand that your shoutout only needs to be up for a few hours to be effective. So when you're negotiating prices a great strategy to use when the Instagram Influencer comes back with their fee is to request only a 6 hour shoutout to cut the cost down some.

Ninja Hack: If you do a shoutout on a big Instagram Influencer page, make a post on your page about 10 to 15 minutes after the Influencer posts your shoutout. You'll be getting a lot of new followers and you want to get in their newsfeed RIGHT AWAY! This gives people enough time for them to follow you and you can immediately drop your content into their newsfeeds. It's not special or fancy, but this one trick has given me a huge boost with my engagement rates.

PURCHASING SHOUTOUTS FOR TRAFFIC

Although growing your follower base is vitally important to your long-term success on Instagram, there is a way you can achieve consistent growth while driving traffic to your website or sales funnel at the same time. This topic is by far where I see most people go wrong and it's also the topic that I get the most questions about. So you are going to want to read this part slowly and carefully.

Similar to shoutouts that help you grow your page, you simply find an Influencer on Instagram in your niche that has a massive community and get them to promote your service or product directly. You aren't focused on followers though – you aren't promoting your brand, rather, you are using them as promotional partners so that you can get your product/service/business in front of the right people for more sales, clients, leads, emails and profits.

After years of hard work, and consistently providing free value, many Instagram Influencers have built massive communities. The Influencers have trust, loyalty and credibility built with their followers. Many of the people who follow these large pages look to the Instagram page owner with celebrity status. They have thousands and thousands of people who are not only interested in following their page for the value the Instagram Influencer provides but are also willing to take it a step further.

The Influencer's followers are actively looking for solutions to their problems and if you choose the right pages to promote with you can easily market your products or services (solutions) directly to their community. If you structure your promotions effectively (more on that in the following chapters) you can collect emails, generate leads, sell your products and generate consistent profits.

The huge advantage you have when choosing to market your products or services directly through Influencer promotions is two fold:

1.   You create an instant spike of traffic to your website or sales funnel which will result in the collection of emails, leads and/or sales. At the very least, you will be able to test your website or sales funnel in only a few hours and use the data to improve your overall conversion rates.

2.   You are still promoting your Instagram brand therefore you will grow your follower base at the same rate, if not faster than if you chose to

promote just your page instead of a product or service.

Simply put, if you choose to promote your page with an Influencer and you purchase a shoutout you will gain followers. But if you choose to promote a product or service you will gain the same, if not more followers and you will be growing your email list, generating leads and making sales. The direct monetization aspect of promoting your products or services with Influencers should not be ignored which is why I consider this strategy to be the most powerful way of building your business on Instagram.

When you are selecting an Influencer to promote your products or services, make sure you choose one who has a large following. Getting someone who only has 50,000 followers will not be very effective. You should be looking for Instagram accounts who have at least 100,000 followers or more, anything less will not drive much traffic to your website or sales funnel nor will it get you many followers. On occasions, you can use smaller pages for quickly testing your promotions/shoutouts. This gives you the ability to make adjustments to your website or sales funnel before you commit large sums of money to your promotions. This is a great way to start out with your first few shoutouts and it can perhaps turn into a partnership once the Instagram account grows in size.

You can also expect to pay slightly more for the Instagram Influencers who put the link to your website or sales funnel directly in their bio. Although this adds an extra cost to the promotion, I have found this to be the best strategy because it increases the amount of traffic to your website or sales funnel dramatically (as much as 314%).

Once you have a selling process that is converting the Instagram followers of pages who have 100,000 to 300,000 followers into buyers, reach out to Instagram pages that have around 500,000 to 800,000 followers. Pages this size on Instagram should send about 500 to 700 visitors to your website or sales funnel and get you about 200 to 300 followers on your own Instagram account. When you purchase promotions from Instagram accounts this size you can expect to pay about $60 for a shoutout that does not have your link in the Instagram Influencers bio and about $85 when your link is placed in the Influencers bio.

Instagram Influencers who have a million followers or more can be expensive to buy shoutouts from. However, these large Instagram pages will give you the best return on your investment when your website or sales funnel is fully optimized and converting visitors into customers. You will receive the most amount of traffic and you will make back many times more than what you paid for the promotion/shoutout. These larger pages have higher credibility and many of the smaller pages' followers will follow the large Instagram pages as well so you'll have a better chance of doubling, tripling or even quadrupling your investment when you promote with these large Instagram pages (as long as your sales funnel is con-verting...more on that in chapter 21).

When you are testing shoutouts and promotions for the first time, you want to post on several different Instagram Influencer pages. All you do here is provide the Influencers you are promoting with the SAME message and the SAME photo. Make certain you do not run a shoutout at the same time on multiple pages and if you do, be sure to use tracking software that will allow you to gage how each shoutout performed (later in this book we will discuss ways to track your promotions). That way you know who to buy more from and who to buy less from or which pages to avoid working with altogether.

CONNECTING WITH INSTAGRAM INFLUENCERS

Your ability to set up profitable promotions that drive traffic to your page and your website or sales funnel will depend on your ability to connect with and partner with the right Instagram Influencers. You must first determine if they are willing to promote your page, product or service. The majority of time, when these Influencers are promoting something you'll see it right away when you read their bio. You can also see if they are sharing other brand's content on their page which is a good indication that they might be open to a shoutout partnership or be willing to sell you shoutouts for your page, product or service.

INSTAGRAM MARKET RESEARCH

Before you can even assess an Instagram Influencer's page to discover if they might be open to promoting your brand, product or service you must identify which communities on Instagram will resonate with you and your brand. This is vitally important to your overall strategy, especially if you are promoting your product or service directly since you must take more critical steps in order to maximize your traffic.

Which market is your brand, product or service best suited for? Use the search function to input search terms

travel / lifestyle
influencer
fashion
art
photog

that are relevant to your business and your niche. You will inevitably find big communities within your market.

However, you don't want to get too focused with this because 'niches' on Instagram can be far more broad than you might expect. For example, motivational pages can attract network marketers, entrepreneurs, business owners and many diverse groups of people. When in doubt, put yourself in your customer's shoes and try to see what pages they would follow. You might have to do some research if you are having trouble with this step but trust me, it will be well worth it.

Focus on collecting a wide range of smaller pages and larger pages. The smaller pages will be ideal for shoutout-for-shoutout partnerships since they will prob-ably be around the same size as your page. They can even be used as test runs for when you start promoting your product or service since you will pay a much lower price when compared to the bigger pages.

Once you have finished your market research and have a few pages you would like to promote with you will want to reach out to these large Instagram pages. They will typically have some contact information in their bio – email or KIK (Warning: Their Instagram username might be different from their KIK name). Sometimes you can direct message (DM) them although most Instagram Influencers don't read their direct messages.

If you are interested in finding shoutout-for-shoutout partners you can simply send them a personal mes-sage and see if they are interested in working with you. If you are looking to expand your partnerships by using shoutout groups the same logic applies – send a per-sonal message to 15 active Instagram accounts. You want anywhere between 10 to 15 people per shoutout group.

When you're reaching out to Instagram Influencers to purchase shoutouts always begin the conversation with a sincere compliment about their page and the content they provide. Ask them for their pricing and their packages (if they have any). Something simple like "Hey, I love your IG page and was wondering if you offered paid shoutouts and if so, what are your rates?" will suffice. Or, you can ask them if they are open for a shoutout-for-shoutout (S4S) if your following is similar to theirs. Always remember: Short, sweet and simple is best.

Be yourself and see if you can negotiate the price down. Remember, they are selling air. Let the Instagram Influencer know if the shoutout you purchase from them is successful you would be willing to purchase 5 or 10 more if they could work with you on the price a bit. However, try not to haggle too much on this. They are spending their time and effort to help you out. Also, never assume they will give you a shoutout free of charge. Your default assumption should be that you are going to have to pay for it.

FAKE INSTAGRAM ACCOUNTS

It's vitally important that you separate the real Instagram accounts from the fake ones. Yes, there are people out there who will buy fake followers to give off the impression of size and shortcut their way to growth. You must be extremely cautious before you get into a shoutout partnership (S4S), join a shoutout group or invest money into a paid shoutout. This is going to require some research where you will have to rely on some key metrics.

A free tool that you should be using is SocialBlade. com. Get used to hearing this name often because it will become your best friend when you are purchasing shoutouts.

What Social Blade allows you to do is plug in an Instagram account and look at their REAL stats. You will get all kinds of details about their follower base and their growth over a longer period of time. If you go to "Detailed Stats," you can see the day-by-day for the last 30 days of their follower growth. With the hourly updates Social Blade offers, you will be able to get a real-time perspective of where your page stands along with where an Instagram Influencers page stands as well.

Tools like SocialBlade.com and FollowerCheck.co are available online and will allow you to see in-depth data of almost any Instagram page and the best part is, they are absolutely free.

There are several things you need to look for BEFORE you purchase a shoutout, but here are six in particular that need to catch your attention:

1. AVERAGE 'LIKE' ACTIVITY:

The average amount of likes over the last 10 posts divided by the total number of followers. 1.5 to 2 percent is the number you are looking for if the Instagram page has over one million followers. For Instagram pages that have less than a million followers the percentage should be much higher: 3 to 7 percent. Anything under these percentages is unfavorable. For best results, skip the first three photos that you see and use the 10 photos after them. Skip any promotions or advertisements and go on to the next photo. Newer posts might not have their usual level of engagement due to the fact that they were recently posted. Comments are not reliable due to continuous changes in Instagram's algorithm and the large amount of "Like & Comment" groups that exist on Instagram. However, if you look through the comments and see a lot of genuine comments that are really engaging with the post that is always a good sign.

2. Excessive promotions:

If you see a lot of ads on an Instagram Influencers page, stay away from them. This could negatively impact your brand and will likely lessen the impact of your promotion/shoutout.

3. Legitimate follower growth over the past 30 days:

BEFORE you ever buy a promotion or a shoutout you must check the page on SocialBlade.com first. Do not send anyone money without thoroughly checking them out. I cannot stress this enough! The amount of people who waste money on Instagram shoutouts is mind-boggling. Do not skip this vital step. (Yes, that was a short rant)

When you are checking a page on Social Blade you want to see consistent and steady growth, day in and day out. If you see thousands of new followers one day followed by next to no growth or even negative growth the next day, stay away. This is a red flag! And it's a sure sign that they are ineffectively growing their page by buying followers. Also watch out for pages that have plateaued. This is a sign that they stopped implementing the strategies that made them successful initially. This illustrates that they are no longer able to grow and most likely have lost the connection they once had with their follower base. For this reason alone, you are highly advised to avoid purchasing accounts from other people on Instagram.

4. AD NETWORKS/GROUPS:

These are people who will reach out to you and promise that your promotion will reach millions of followers. They conveniently forget to tell you that these 'millions of followers' comprise of several smaller groups (100,000 followers each or less) and they are always giving each other shoutouts so in essence you are getting in front of the exact same followers on each Instagram page. They fall under red flag #2 and you will end up paying more to reach the same group of followers. Learn from my experience – I have never had good results with this strategy.

5. MULTIPLE PAGE OWNERS:

They are similar to red flag #4 in that they give shoutouts to the same pages which in turn has them acquiring the same followers on each page. If you choose to work with them, focus exclusively on only working with their page that has the highest number of followers.

6. ACTIVITY:

Go through the most recent 3 posts and check the date and time when they were posted. If these 3 posts are old (2 days or later), the Instagram account can be considered to be somewhat inactive. However, if these 3 posts were all posted within a 24 hour period, that is a sign of high activity. Although it may be tempting to promote with Instagram pages who only post once or twice a week because their engagement on their post is generally higher than the ones who post more frequently, I advise you to not do it. I have tested this and never achieved good results from pages who don't post at least 3 times a day.

Update: I've recently noticed that some Instagram accounts are making their account private to avoid Social Blade tracking. This is a way they can deceive people into believing they have more followers than they actually do. When someone makes an Instagram account private Social Blade stops tracking its growth (this is why you should never make your Instagram account private). I advise you to not form partnerships with Instagram pages that you cannot track on Social Blade.

Once you have narrowed your list of potential Influencers to partner with and they have passed the 6 steps listed above, you will want to reach out to these large Instagram pages and set up your shoutout promotions. Start small with one or two partners and begin testing your promotions. If you are purchasing shoutouts from Instagram Influencers, make sure to start with one promotional post only and try to get a "Trial" discount. You want to test your audience before you buy larger packages and invest larger sums of money.

No matter what strategy you are using (shoutout partnerships, paid shoutouts for growth or paid shoutouts for traffic to your website or sales funnel) your goal should be to find a few Influencers that you can trust and continually use for promotions. Just 5 to 6 core partners are really all you need to put this system on autopilot.

Once you have Influencers promoting your brand you will begin to see a steady flow of people following you, engaging with your content and if you have a website or sales funnel, you will receive a continuous flow of traffic resulting in leads, emails and sales. Soon enough you will have your own community of followers that you can deliver value and promote to on a consistent basis without having to rely on partnerships and paid shout-outs. That should be your ultimate goal on Instagram.

CHAPTER 11

Throwing Gasoline On the Fire: How To Nurture Your Community & Leverage Engagement Groups

As you begin to implement the strategies outlined in this book thus far, you're follower base should be growing at a very consistent rate. The momentum that you will begin to experience must be maintained at all costs. Consistent daily actions (the right actions) done over time will naturally produce consistent results (the right results). Day in and day out you must be engaging with and building your community.

Take a look at what the massive Instagram pages do. They treat their communities like a garden that is watered and nurtured daily. Multiple times a day, they tend to their garden and ensure that it is growing at a steady pace. Cultivating relationships with your followers is where a majority of your efforts need to be focused.

Successful pages will post valuable and empowering content multiple times a day. They will actively engage with their followers numerous times a day. When Instagram users see that a page genuinely cares for them and personally reaches out to them, that provides a huge incentive for other followers to engage. You will see that your community eventually becomes a self-engaging machine that you can easily promote your products and services to and chances are they will be grateful for it.

There are multiple ways by which you can build influence and increase your engagement by connecting with current and potential followers. Here are the most basic ways by which this is done. More advanced strategies will be discussed later:

Sharing: You can share your followers' photos on your page (make sure you ask for permission first) and spread their name around. Better yet, share content if their photo features your product, brand or service in it. This is a great way to go the extra mile and show that you really care about your loyal fans!

Liking: What better way to show people you care than to like their photos? When you start liking photos, people will see that you are interested in being part of a community. You won't be perceived as someone who takes and takes without giving anything back.

Commenting: This is where you can really kick things up a notch and develop a connection with Instagram users. Comment on the photos posted by your followers and by those you follow. Say something that compliments their post and always be sincere in your message. Mention them by tagging their @username for bonus points!

Messaging: Using simple call to action messages in

your images and captions will get people to like your post and share it with people who they think will agree with your message. It can be funny or serious as long as it is relevant to your brand and your niche. Simple "Double Tap If You Agree" or "Tag Someone Who: Motivates You, Inspires You, Is Going To Be A Millionaire" will produce extremely high engagement rates as long as it is relatable to your followers and their friends.

Following: You didn't think that you were going to be able to do all of this without following other people, did you? Follow the people who follow you if possible but don't worry about following everybody. There is something to be said about having a small amount of pages that you follow and if you study successful pages within your niche, you should see a number that is reasonable that you can model.

Return Direct Messages: Being bombarded with direct messages from your followers can seem overwhelming at times. However, you must remember that your followers will eventually become your customers. Therefore it is vital that you do not neglect their direct messages and you are constantly checking your "requested" messages from Instagram users who are not directly connected with you.

Use the stories feature to highlight positive direct messages you received: Something a lot of the top Instagram Influencers are doing lately is taking screenshots of the direct messages they receive from their followers which shows their exchange in communication and posting them on their stories feature. This shows their followers that they are actively engaging with their community which encourages more people to engage with them.

Use the stories feature to show your new post: A great way to use your Instagram stories feature is to take a screenshot of your Instagram profile and use Instagram drawing capabilities to block out your most recent post. Type new over the post and that will encourage people to go check out your profile.

Contest & Giveaways: This is a great growth hacking strategy that will increase engagement amongst your current followers while attracting new ones to your page. There's nothing people love more than a contest where they have a chance to win FREE stuff. Your audience will grow while your brand awareness improves. You kill two birds with one stone. You don't even have to give away anything expensive, although you could if you wanted to. Things like subscriptions or one of your products for free are already great incentives for people to enter your online challenge. A copy of your brand new book, one of your hottest items in your store – be creative. You can even create a hashtag that is unique to your brand. Have your followers use the hashtag and spread it around wherever they can. Engage with the people who use your hashtag by replying with a comment. This encourages more people to use it since they know they are more likely to get a response from you. This is not something that you want to do when you are new to Instagram. You are far better off waiting until you have at least a few thousand followers. Because there's no point in catering to an audience that doesn't exist yet.

ENGAGEMENT GROUPS

Another great way to foster engagement on your Instagram posts is through "like and comment" groups. This is similar to shoutout groups except you are going to be liking and commenting on other people's posts and in return, your posts will receive likes and comments therefore increasing the overall engagement on your posts. Like the shoutout trains, you can recruit other pages via direct message on Instagram until you have a group of 15.

Reach out to accounts that have a similar size to yours and don't be shy to reach out to larger accounts as well. Just make sure that their engagement rates are solid. You can always join my private Facebook group that is dedicated to connecting Instagrammers to quality like and comment groups:

https://www.facebook.com/groups/IGLikeComment/)

When other members of your Instagram "like and comment" group comment on your posts, their followers are going to gain access to your content. When you are under 100,000 followers, this is a great strategy to use so that you can grow your follower base fast. The sooner everyone begins engaging with each other's content, the greater the opportunity you have of appearing in the "Explore" page on Instagram. On this page, ALL of the 650,000,000+ users on Instagram will have a chance to see your Instagram post. You expose yourself to more people, you get more followers, and the rest speaks for itself.

Certain Instagram "like and comment" groups use specific hashtags to connect. Later in this book you will learn more about this opportunity and much more about using hashtags effectively.

If you decide to join a "like and comment" group just make sure that you are timely with your engagement in these groups. You want to like and comment on the group members' photos as soon as possible (they need to do the same for you). Keep in mind, one of the hardest things in life is getting people to work together so inevitably you might be faced with having an engagement group that doesn't engage much.

These engagement groups work best when everyone cooperates and participates so it's vital that you add as much value as you can by liking members of the group's Instagram posts quickly once they are posted and avoid leaving generic comments. The more sincere you are, the more engagement the other participants in the group will give you. This ultimately benefits you in several ways: More followers, better comments, and more leads and sales.

A downside with engagement groups is the fact that you must rely on other people's efforts in order for your own efforts to be rewarded, so be cautious of who you allow in your group. An easier way to ensure that you have the right people in your group is to use Telegram engagement groups.

THE POWER OF TELEGRAM

Telegram is a free app you can download that allows you to create, organize, and moderate groups of people which makes it a powerful tool for not only setting up engagement groups, but for managing them as well. The best part is, there are already countless people using this app to create engagement groups specifically for Instagram and it has proven to be an extremely effective strategy.

Telegram essentially operates in the same way as a "like and comment" group. However, the primary difference is Telegram groups focus more on something called "rounds". Rounds are mainly focused on liking other Instagram users posts rather than commenting on them because likes currently play a higher role in Instagrams algorithm for deciding who's Instagram post gets added to the Explore page.

Many of these groups are private and typically there's a fee to join. There are also groups for Instagram users who have a particular amount of followers. For example: There are telegram groups for Instagram users who have 10k, 50k, 100k, 500k followers and above.

To join a Telegram group you have to meet various requirements: First you need to have access to the private Telegram group's unique link. You can get this secret link by finding someone who can send it to you. Another way to gain access is to locate a groups admin and message them directly. Obviously this requires finding the right people. Once you have access to a Telegram group you will want to review the pinned post showing the rules and explaining how the group works. Practically every group has a pinned post so it's vital you review it so you know exactly what will be expected of you and how that specific group operates.

Inside each of these Telegram engagement groups is where "rounds" take place. The purpose of a "round" is to game Instagram's algorithm by getting as much engagement as possible within the first hour of posting. The faster your posts receives likes and comments the higher the probability your content will reach not only more of your own followers but have a greater chance of making it to Instagram's Explore page.

Here is a simple 3 step process that Telegram groups

follow to ensure that each "round" is effective in pro-viding everyone with a high level of engagement on their Instagram posts:

Step 1: 30 minutes before the round starts, the host/admin will prompt you to drop your Instagram username into the group.

Step 2: Host/admin compiles all the Instagram user-names into a list, then at the specified time of the round (usually at 9am EST, 12pm EST, 3pm EST and 9pm EST) gives everyone 60 to 120 minutes depending on the group's rules to engage on the most recent Instagram post of those who are participating in that round.

Step 3: You must engage with all the Instagram users who are participating in the round by liking their most recent posts within the specified time the Telegram group requires. Failure to do so will get you blacklisted from the group.

Telegram groups use an automated system that checks directly on Instagram whether or not you gave likes so it's vital that you fully participate and adhere to the group's rules.

People who don't engage back with others in the group are called 'leechers' and there is a 'leecher' detector in each group that will find the people who do not engage and will warn them. After several warnings they will be removed from the group. Since the entire purpose of using this strategy is to ensure everyone is engaging back the group's leecher detector plays a vital role in moderating the group and making sure everyone involved is actively participating.

If you get banned from a Telegram group you can get

back in by messaging the administrator and following their "unbanned account" process which typically results in a few days of being banned or you might have to pay an unban fee.

The first week I participated in a the "rounds" on Telegram I increased my engagement by over 800 likes per post so this is definitely a strategy worth considering if you are looking to increase your engagement and build your community.

DON'T FORGET ABOUT THE FUNDAMENTALS

Engagement groups are a great way to game Instagram's algorithm and get your posts in front of millions of Instagram users. However, do not focus so much on the fancy stuff ("rounds") that you forget about the fundamentals (engaging with your followers).

I see a lot of people on Instagram so hungry to get their next new follower that they neglect the followers they currently have. Never get so focused on growth that you forget about the followers you currently have. Return their DMs. Thank them for their comments. Go and like a few of their Instagram posts.

Engaging with your followers may seem simple but it will provide you with a massive return on your investment over time if you stick with it. Because not only will you have a large community of raving fans, but you will also have a LOYAL community of raving fans. This strong relationship you will have built with your followers will then translate into trust where you can offer them your products and services that meet their needs.

Understand that virtually every Instagram user has a

problem that needs to be solved. And if you can earn their loyalty and trust, then position your product or service to solve their problem – not only will you be able to profit; you will also be able to enrich your followers lives. Growing a large Instagram following comes with a price, and that price is being someone your followers can look to for answers.

CHAPTER 12

Scroll Stopping Images: Advanced Post Creation Strategies To Increase Engagement, Follower Loyalty & Sales

By now, it should be extremely obvious that Instagram relies entirely on attractive visual content. However, there is an art and science to posting photos that will attract followers and increase engagement. You don't want your photos to repel people away from your Instagram page, do you?

You might feel somewhat limited at first because the primary source of content on Instagram is simply images. What you might not realize is that within this single medium you have an infinite amount of possibilities. There are so many ways in which you can touch people's hearts and establish yourself as a credible authority in your niche. It takes only one picture to elicit an emotion that attracts a new follower to you and compels them to engage. Now is the time to think outside the box and break past the traditional rules. Every single post should be perceived as an opportunity to connect with your community and encourage them to take some kind of action: Like, comment, tag or share.

This chapter is packed with tips on how to use the power of visual imagery to provide more value to your followers while increasing the success that you have with your own promotions and advertisements. Let's dive in!

HIGH-QUALITY

Thanks to the rapid advances of photo technology in the 21st century, the minimum requirements for quality are higher than ever. Everyone is going on Instagram with the expectation that every photo will be clean and crisp. It only takes one crappy-looking image for people to scroll down their newsfeed and forget about your post instantly. I've done the testing and this has held true in every single experiment. Trust me on this one.

Moreover, if you are doing a shoutout with a major Instagram Influencer, how do you think it will make them look if they share one of your low-quality images? You are hurting your brand, but more importantly you are hurting THEIR brand. Do not skip this part. Invest in a high-quality camera, use photo-editing software – do whatever it takes to ensure each and every photo is of stellar quality.

DIGITAL PRODUCT SELLERS: LEARN FROM THE PHYSICAL PRODUCT SELLERS

Have you ever seen how physical products are marketed on Instagram? By physical products, I mean things like watches, cars, shirts and other physical items. Many of the major businesses and brands on Instagram are making killer profits by leveraging the strategies I talked about in chapter 10.

How does this apply to you? Well, let's say that you have a digital product that you want to sell. It could be a program, a video course, an ebook, or anything that can be accessed on an electronic device.

Instead of posting the digital picture that has been edited to look real, take a picture of the product in its physical form and use that as your promotional photo. An ebook would be presented as a physical book. Print the cover out and tape the ebook cover to a physical book or a magazine. An audio course would be presented as multiple labelled CDs (or the CD cover could be shown on an iPhone screen). A video course could be presented as several DVD cases or even a picture of an iPad with the cover designed on the screen.

It sounds silly until you try it for yourself. I noticed that traffic to my sales funnels skyrocketed after implementing this strategy. As a result, my profits were substantially higher and creating shoutouts/promotions has never been easier. What better way for an Influencer to show that they personally recommend your product than them having a physical form of it?

When you're designing an image for an Instagram Influencer to post on their page, make sure that the book (or DVD/CD) stands out as the HIGHLIGHT of the picture. It needs to be visible and directly in front of the customer's face.

To take this to the next level, <u>make your shoutout/promotion look more native</u>. Take a picture of your ebook (remember, print the cover out and tape it to a physical book) alongside other bestselling books that are currently in your niche. Another strategy that has worked great for me is to take a photo of your ebook by common items like a laptop, phone, watch, or anything else that you think will add more authenticity to the picture.

You will have to try out different variations to see which ones generate the highest amount of traffic to your website or sales funnel. Continue to test and analyze your results. Eventually you'll begin to collect emails like crazy and generate predictable profits with this ninja strategy.

There were three promotions/shoutouts of mine that were mega hits and gave me extraordinary results.

One shoutout involved putting my book at the forefront of a collection of other books within my niche that were extremely well known. This got me great traffic and amazing engagement. It also converted at an unbelievable rate of 72% when I used it to collect email addresses and up to 18% when I sold it for $4.97.

The second variation involved a 1-page excerpt of the actual book printed out, with a memorable quote. People can see that it's a real product and my engagement went through the roof!

The third promotion/shoutout had the physical appearance of the book and the table of contents printed out alongside the book. People got a free sneak peek of the book and this builds up anticipation for what's inside of the book.

Don't worry if people think it's a physical product – if it's entirely digital, you can inform them of this on your sales page. My refund rates are very low in spite of this (lower than 2%) and these strategies have not failed me to date.

When it comes to promoting your digital products you need to see what works and what people actually engage with. You will constantly need to be analyzing and adjusting your Instagram ads. But one of the best things about Instagram is that you really only need to spend about $200 to fine tune your shoutout promotions.

NON-INFORMATION PRODUCTS

This is referring to physical products like clothing, watches, health supplements and so on. Here, high definition photos are key and you may have to hire a professional photographer to get these created.

For products that can be worn, I've found that adding a human element to the promotion (a person wearing the shirt, a wrist featuring a bracelet, etc.) provides greater engagement (and higher conversions) compared to a photo where the item is being displayed in isolation.

I've also found that it is best to keep words on the photo to a minimum. At some point there is too much going on in the photo and it becomes unappealing to the Instagram viewer. This was reflected in lower engagement that my text-heavy photos received. Remember, you have just a second at best to catch someone's attention on Instagram so you don't want to overwhelm them with flashy promotions loaded with text.

For example, I have noticed that brief yet effective motivational quotes increase engagement. Of course, this depends on the niche because some niches are not suited for quotes.

Some successful ads that I've seen on Instagram have used extremely bold calls to action. Test your photos with bold calls to action and with subtle ones as well to see which ones convert best.

You want to stage a native environment but not at the expense of being unable to decipher the message or taking any attention away from the product you are trying to sell. You want a healthy mix of nativity and marketing in your photo.

In general, I've seen that having too much going on in a shoutout/promotion leads to low engagement with regards to likes, comments and sales. This distracts the potential buyer and takes away from your overall objective: Selling the product. Don't put so much text or do a ton of graphic editing to the point where the main message gets buried.

Ninja Hack: Show your product off at multiple angles. You can even combine multiple images staged into a single frame. Some of the most successful photos in the fashion and accessory niches have employed this technique for better engagement and higher conversions on their sales page. And with Instagram's new feature that allows you to upload multiple images to a single post, this gives your potential buyers a lot of variety that can encourage them to purchase your product!

SERVICE-BASED

Remember how you don't want to have too much editing in photos promoting physical products? I'm going to do a 180 here and encourage you to make the necessary edits to drive home the benefits your service-based business provides. However, you want to strike the right balance: The photos can't blend in too much to the surrounding posts but you also want them to stand out. Avoid standing out too much because you don't want to stick out like a sore thumb.

This isn't my specialty, so it will be up to you to do a lot of testing in this area. Try out different styles, look at pages promoting services and see which promotions were most successful. The engagement rates will tell you everything that you need to know.

TAKE IT EASY ON COLORS

Your Instagram promotions need to be visual and attractive. That does not mean that you should be recreating the rainbow with each and every photo that you post. In fact, I've found that sticking to a single dominant color results in far more engagement. Moreover, when you make that single dominant color a 'cool' color (teal, titanium, etc.), the engagement goes up even higher! That was just my personal experience – play around with colors and see what happens. Maybe your photos will have a higher like count if you use warm colors like blue. You will just have to test it out and see.

THE TWO-THIRDS RULE

The product or person featuring the product should occupy no more than two-thirds of the total shot. This allows the product to be dominant while providing enough space around it to fully process the object. This leads to more compelling photos with a higher level of engagement. Most smartphones have a grid function that will allow you to easily execute this.

FILTER IT BABY!

Filters aren't only used to make poor photos look better – they are also far more likely to receive high engagement in the form of likes and comments. In particular, the warmer filters perform best. One exception: Avoid filters when you are promoting your products. Followers want to see exactly what they are paying money for.

PICK A FONT THAT STANDS OUT

You will have to test different fonts to see which ones produce the best engagement. This tip is particularly important for people who are running pages that are heavy on using quotes as part of their content. You are looking for the following in your font(s) of choice:

- Clear to read
- Can be seen from far distances
- Has aesthetic appeal
- Is not boring, confusing or ugly looking

When the right fonts are chosen text in photos become compelling and engaging. You will probably find that you have a few fonts that work best for your audience in terms of engagement. Test them, find out which ones your followers love and stick with them.

GO PRO

One way to make your Instagram posts more appealing is to apply a professional touch to your photos. Make sure your camera or phone is completely upright when taking pictures. If you are taking pictures from a surface, the camera should be three feet above the object and completely parallel to the surface.

CREATE BACKUPS FOR YOUR PHOTOS AND YOUR CONTENT

Despite the fact that we live in the 21st century, we still have a tendency to fall victim to device failures and crashes. It would be a shame if one unfortunate slip led to the loss of all of your hard work.

It would be to your advantage to set up a system in which you backup all your shared photos onto a spare hard drive or an online storage application like Dropbox, Google Drive or Evernote. Better yet, make it a habit to create a backup of a photo and the caption whenever it is posted on your Instagram page.

Ninja Hack: IFTTT.com can be set to automatically upload your Instagram posts and captions to dropbox as well as many other online storage devices. This can be a great solution for safeguarding all of your hard work.

DON'T POST COLLAGES

Some people try to get fancy and post partial pictures so that they combine into a larger picture when placed side by side. Everything needs to be perfect and the whole thing falls apart when you post a new photo to your page. The simple solution is to avoid using this strategy altogether.

SHARE YOUR PHOTOS ON MULTIPLE SOCIAL MEDIA PLATFORMS

This is only relevant to people whose brand or business is not exclusive to the Instagram platform. There's no point in limiting your visual, engaging and value-adding content to only one social media platform. You can use software programs such as IFTTT and Buffer to distribute your content across multiple social media platforms. You already went through the hard work of creating visually pleasing content – why not get the greatest return on your investment possible from it?

TAKE ADVANTAGE OF PHOTO OPPORTUNITIES

There are multiple ways in which you can provide valuable content to your followers through the photos you post. It might feel like your options are limited, until you sit down and brainstorm all the things that you can post to your page without sacrificing the value that you provide your community on Instagram. Here is a brief list of the things that you can try:

- Show yourself or your team members engaged in activity, whether they are working hard or playing hard.

- Give followers a glimpse into your office – show them what a working day is like in your life.

- Reveal some photos that show your products, digital or physical, in the production phase. This is a great "behind-the-scenes" look that makes your fans feel like they are getting something that nobody else is getting.

- Provide a sneak peek of a hot new product you are about to release to the public. The more subtle you are, the more curiosity you generate in your followers. They'll keep following you in hopes that you reveal that next great thing.

- Post a photo of what your products are capable of doing.

- Give your followers a glimpse into some of the events you attend.

That's a short list to get you started. Depending on your niche, you can probably come up with more. And I want to encourage you to make certain you are using Instagram's "Stories" feature when you are giving your followers "behind the scenes" access to your life. This is an excellent opportunity to post a discount code on your Instagram Story and tell your followers that it's only good for 24 hours.

BE CAREFUL WITH REPOSTING IMAGES

Some people focus exclusively on reposting other people's Instagram content. The main premise here is becoming a page known for aggregating the best content for a certain niche and compiling it into one page for easy access. There is nothing wrong with this, but there are several precautions you need to keep in mind when using this strategy. I'll list them below along with some tips that will help you maximize this technique I see many Instagrammers using these days:

- Avoid screenshots. You are degrading the quality of the image and people will be able to tell right away that you are not providing quality content. There are several applications that will allow you to directly download images and make edits in another application. The app I like to use for downloading Instagram images is called: InsSave.

- Don't steal. You are using other people's content. Give credit to the person who created the original post or took the photo. If you can't find them, create a call to action in the caption for the originator to DM or email you. Giving appropriate credit and having the right permissions helps avoid copyright infringements.

- Don't just use the highest-performing photos. Reposting photos with high engagement rates is the lazy way out and your Instagram page will experience slow growth. If you want to be the place where you collect rare photos, you need to find photos that aren't getting the attention they deserve. This is the counter-intuitive secret to boosting your engagement rate as a reposting page.

- Find photographers to work with. If you search around on Instagram, you can probably find a couple of photographers who are looking to spread their content around. This strategy works better when you have a greater following with high engagement rates because your influence provides an incentive for photographers to work with you.

- • How to recover liked photos for re-sharing: Go to your profile and click "options," and then select "Posts you've liked." You will have access to pictures that you have liked in the past, which can be used for curating valuable content for your followers.

You are now equipped with an endless amount of options for tweaking and customizing your photos to make them stand out on Instagram. If you are starting off, there is a lot of testing to be done in the beginning. It will take a lot of trial and error combined with using SocialBlade.com analytics to find the patterns and trends that work best for growing your audience on Instagram.

As I stated previously in this book, testing on Instagram takes no more than a day (many times only a few hours). You can test different posts as well as shoutouts and see which ones produce the best engagement and sales. You'll be able to quickly analyze and adjust your strategies to zero in on what will be the most effective for achieving your objective.

When it comes to succeeding on Instagram I have learned that we are only as good as the speed at which we can test things out – so try new variations of the strategies you are learning in this book, see what works, and keep making adjustments until you find what gets you the best results!

CHAPTER 13

Instagram Videos: Your Secret Weapon for Engagement, Generating Sales & Going Viral

One of the features that is getting a lot of attention on Instagram is the ability for people to post videos to their account in addition to photos. Introduced in 2013, it quickly became a popular option and there is no sign of that growth slowing down anytime soon.

Initially, there was a 15 second limit on how long your videos could be on Instagram, but now the limit has been removed and your videos can be up to a minute long. This provides users with an endless amount of options for customization and promotion. You can edit your videos and add any filters of your choosing.

Already, many businesses and brands are beginning

to use Instagram videos as a way to engage with their fans and increase their follower base. People no longer have to spend their time on Facebook, Twitter or You-Tube to get access to content packed videos. This is huge for those looking to take their Instagram game to the next level.

With videos, leveraging call-to-actions is a bit harder. Unless people take the time to actually open up your video and watch the entire thing, they are probably going to miss it.

If you have spent any time on the Internet, you probably know how powerful viral videos can be. On any social media platform that you look at, viral videos get far more engagement than an ordinary photo or video. The only thing to remember is that the success of viral videos is measured by the number of views they get. If you have a lot of viral videos on your account, you can expect great long-term growth in return. On Instagram, views work a little differently. The video needs to be watched by the viewer for at least 3 seconds to count as a 'view'.

The unique thing about videos on Instagram is that they have twice as much engagement as photos do in terms of commenting, yet photos have twice as much engagement as videos do in terms of likes.

Videos sell and that is not going to change anytime soon. Here are some tips to take advantage of this under-rated Instagram strategy.:

- Choose a thumbnail that gets high engagement. When you are posting your video, the thumbnail is going to be the frozen part of the video. People are going to see this before clicking the video, meaning that you have to capture their attention right away. Put the exciting stuff in front of their face!

- Choose videos that can potentially go viral and provide you with a high engagement rate: You want to pick videos that your audience can relate to while reaching out to potential followers. This is no different from the content strategy discussed earlier in this book. This means that you want to aim for videos that nobody else has seen yet, these have the best potential to go viral. If you can do this consistently, you will see a lot of success in the form of comments, likes and most importantly new followers.

- Make sure the highlight of the video happens right away. Unlike video sharing on other platforms, you can't skip to a certain part of the video. You have to sit and watch the entire thing until the very end. Making viewers wait is a great way to lower your chances of increased engagement. Nobody who successfully used videos to boost engagement rates on their Instagram page ever failed because they overestimated the patience of their followers!

- When I use videos on Instagram to promote my products and services I always add text on the bottom of the video that says "TAP FOR SOUND." This is important because when an Instagram user is scrolling through their newsfeed they will be able to see your video but not hear it until they tap your Instagram post. Often times I only have the "TAP FOR SOUND" text appear for the first 15 seconds of the video. After that the text disappears.

I don't use a lot of videos on my own Instagram pages, but it is difficult to deny that they are an effective growth hack when used correctly and consistently. Videos are not mandatory and should only be used if they make sense in the context of your particular niche. With that being said, you will get better at making them over time as you practice and test new things out to see which videos get the highest levels of engagement.

Instagram has recently added a feature that allows you to go LIVE which is very similar to Facebook's live streaming feature. The great thing about going live on Instagram is that Instagram notifies all of your followers who are currently on Instagram and tells them you are live. This feature has not received much attention yet, but I guarantee it will increase substantially over the next few years.

Now is the time to get ahead of the curve and begin taking advantage of the Instagram live feature. Connect with your followers and allow them to see you in real-time and in your real form. What do I mean? I think it's extremely important that your followers realize you're a real person, that you're not perfect, and that you are vulnerable enough to allow them to interact with you and your imperfect life.

Ninja Hack: Repurposing your Instagram live videos can also be a great way to spread your content across other social media platforms. Now that Instagram allows you to save your live videos I highly encourage you to do that and then make the video available for your followers who didn't have the opportunity to watch you while you were live.

Videos are by far the best way to communicate a message to your followers. Nothing conveys an idea and allows you to layout the benefits of your products and services like a video will. I understand none of us are good in the beginning when we first start recording videos. But something I have learned is that you don't practice things in life until you get them right, you practice until you can't get them wrong.

When you learn to pitch your products and services using the 60 second timeframe Instagram gives you, you will not only see your follower base engage with you more than ever before, you'll also see your sales skyrocket.

CHAPTER 14

How To Write Captions That Get Your Followers To Take ACTION

Here is where the selling gets fun! Now that you have optimized your photos and your plan for expanding your follower base by leveraging Instagram Influencers, it's time to put your copywriting hat on and craft a compelling caption.

Your caption is the text that goes below your image. This is where you can deliver your own written message that expands upon the image in your post. If you are promoting something, this is your chance to explain to the followers on the page you are promoting on (or on your own page) what they should do. In the caption of your Instagram post you need to tell people what they should click on and what benefits they will receive from doing so. This is where you provide a strong call-to-action and sell them on why they should visit your website or sales funnel and buy your product or service.

One of the keys to a high-converting caption is to keep things short and sweet. People are not going to hit "more" and read the rest of your caption unless you lure them in with a strong opening sentence or two. Remember that you are dealing with customers on a mobile platform that have hundreds of other posts they could be engaging with.

The best way to maximize the text in your caption is to focus solely on the benefits (NOT THE FEATURES). You focus on what your followers (or the Instagram Influencer's followers) are going to get when they click your link. Try to answer these questions: What's in it for them? Why is your promotion worth their limited attention in the first place?

You also want to write the caption as if it was a personal message. It can't read like some aggressive over-hyped sales pitch. Instagram users will see right through it and perceive your copy as fake and inauthentic. When you focus on a more conversational tone, it sounds like it is coming from a real person who genuinely cares about their success. This is especially important when you are promoting on an Instagram Influencer's page and their followers are reading the caption. The Influencer's followers need to feel like the Influencer wrote the caption themselves and is personally endorsing your product or service. This is crucial to a successful promotion/ shoutout.

When an Instagram Influencer is promoting your product on their page you want to make it seem like they are recommending your product because they want to, not because you are paying them to do so. This should stand out in the first two sentences of the promotion/ shoutout and it should sound as genuine as possible.

At the same time, you do want to sell the person on visiting your website or sales funnel. That's why you made the promotion in the first place, right? Your personal approach got people to start reading but now you want them to stay glued to your caption. And what you write next in the caption is going to largely depend on the product you are selling. Below, I've taken the liberty to provide you with some examples that I've seen work great on Instagram when it comes to writing a compelling caption.

PHYSICAL PRODUCTS

Discounts and limited time offers are great for creating a sense of urgency for your potential customer. Everyone loves a good deal when they get it before other shoppers do. If you can afford it, free shipping is another great incentive. "Free worldwide shipping", "Discount code at X% for a limited time only" are great examples of captions that get Instagram users to take action and buy your product.

DIGITAL PRODUCTS

Presell your product by listing a benefit or two. People want to know how they can benefit and what they can expect to achieve before they spend their time visiting your website. Also, giving FREE bonuses is a great strategy for adding value and persuading people to take action and purchase your product.

If you put the price of your product or service in your caption, you can expect less traffic but a higher number of conversions on your website or sales funnel. I personally like the strategy of letting people know the price immediately – because when people click on your link they know in advance that they are going to have to pay for something.

If you are promoting something FREE, make sure you mention the word "free" at least once. Everyone loves a free product! People also love the words 'bonuses' and "gifts."

Ninja Hack: If you can place the word FREE in the URL of the link the Instagram user will be clicking it will increase traffic to your website or sales funnel drastically: YourProduct.com/FREE

One of my main strategies is to offer an ebook for $4.97 that comes with a free audiobook, so in the caption I mention the price by saying "and at only $4.97 it's an absolute no-brainer" and I mention the fact they get a FREE audiobook as well. This allows me to hit on both the upfront mention of the price along with the word free.

Remember, if you are promoting on an Instagram Influencers page the caption should be written as though the Influencer is personally recommending your product which helps you frame the price and the free offer effectively.

You will have to test captions where you state the price and where you don't to see what works best for you. Continue to A/B test multiple captions until you find what converts the highest. My experience is that the tactics above generate the most profits.

After the sales message, add in another sentence or two that reinforces the personal Instagram Influencer's recommendation. This keeps you from going into a super-aggressive sales pitch and reminds people that this product is a genuine recommendation directly from the page owner, which again is vital.

Last but not least, the famous call-to-action. Here, you are instilling urgency and telling followers EXACTLY what needs to be done right now. You want to direct people to your link AND your Instagram page. Throw in the URL if you can and your @InstagramName at the end of the call to action. This gets people to go to your link while reminding them to follow you!

More money AND more traffic to your Instagram page – that's killing two birds with one stone therefore accelerating your overall success.

Let's recap: Personal message to grab their attention, selling 1 to 2 benefits to keep them hooked, reinforcement of the Instagram Influencers recommendation/ endorsement, call-to-action along with telling followers to follow you if you are promoting on a page that is not your own.

A simple 4 to 5 sentence framework that is easy to remember works every time. Don't be afraid to continually change your message around until you get the best results.

Note: A new strategy I have been testing out recently is to open the caption with a question. This behaves as a pattern interrupt and gets your reader thinking.

Once you get this outline down, it's extremely easy to create compelling captions and you wonder why you did not think of this tactic sooner. Often times it's the simplest things in marketing that lead to dramatic increases in traffic and profits.

Even if you aren't trying to sell something, a compelling and engaging caption about a picture that you post can increase your engagement significantly. I've found that longer captions (not too long) have more people tagging others compared to captions that only contain a few words. You can add even more value and more of a personal touch to your followers with a great caption. You establish trust and build a relationship with your followers where you are perceived as a credible authority that consistently delivers massive value when you provide them with concise – yet captivative captions. This virtually guarantees that more people will follow you, visit your website and buy your products and services.

You will know when you have the right caption in place when people are compelled to do more than view your picture and scroll up. Sharing the post, commenting and liking are just some of the many ways that they can engage with you. You want to ENCOURAGE people to naturally and effortlessly engage – it must not feel like a chore to them.

CHAPTER 15

The Hashtag Lie: Why More Is NOT Better, How To Find the Right Ones & How Many To Use

Ah, this is the part that you were probably wondering about. With so many people using hashtags all the time on Instagram, they must be super important. Right?

Wrong!

There's actually a hard limit on the amount of hashtags that you should be using. And just because you can post up to 30 hashtags on a picture does not mean that you should. Here is what happens if you go down this route:

Sure, you'll get lots of new followers and an increased amount of likes. You must be getting greater engagement. Not so fast! For one, you are going to attract automation bots that are specifically programmed to like or follow people who post using a certain hashtag. This dilutes your following of engaged followers and decreases your engagement rate over the long-term which annihilates your chances of consistently making it to the Explore page on Instagram. Additionally, you are attracting people that might not see your posts or page, let alone be interested in the niche that you cater to.

In short, using excessive hashtags is just a game of improving your likes and followers for the sake of having higher numbers. If you recall from earlier discussions in this book, you know that more followers does not necessarily lead to more dollars in your bank account. The primary focus of this entire book is to walk you through step-by-step how to generate predictable profits from your Instagram page. And in order to do that successfully you have to create a community of real and engaged followers that genuinely want your content. You cannot develop a loyal follower base by pasting 30 hashtags on each of your Instagram posts.

If you look at my page (ElevateYourMindset) along with other large Instagram pages, you'll quickly notice that hashtags are rarely used. On the occasion that they are used, they are either specific to the post or their overall brand.

The maximum number of hashtags you will see on large Instagram Influencer pages is 5, with 1 to 3 being the norm. Since hashtags lead to engagement from people who don't even see the post, you cannot know when you are receiving true engagement. This is why you should strive to leave any hashtags off of your content when you are testing new and different content strategies.

Leave the game of hashtag oversaturation to people who don't understand the concept of acquiring real and engaged followers. Go the opposite direction and get real engagement that you can utilize to accurately track your growth. With that said, there is no need to completely demonize hashtags. Used sparingly and strategically, they can be yet another useful tool in your arsenal for increasing your follower base and your engagement. Here are some tips for using hashtags on your Instagram page effectively.

BE SPECIFIC

The most successful Instagram Influencers only use targeted hashtags or ones specific to their brand. You want to model that same approach. Using generic and spam hashtags (anything with a '4' in it) will hurt engagement in the long run because you will be unfollowed for not engaging back through commenting or following them.

Plus, your followers aren't going to your page so that they can be spammed with endless hashtags in each photo. It looks out of place and some of your followers will get the impression that you are a bot-run spam page.

KEEP HASHTAGS IN THE COMMENTS

This ensures that your picture will be found when a particular hashtag is entered into the search field. It makes your content more accessible to those who are searching for your hashtag but are not following you.

Moreover, your caption is for valuable sales copy that gets people to take action (follow someone, click on the link in the bio, etc.). Don't take up valuable space with distracting hashtags. You can fix this by putting the hashtags in as a comment on the post. Just because this is so important I want to repeat this point and make it crystal clear: DO NOT put hashtags in the caption section of your Instagram post. Put your hashtags in as a comment on your Instagram post.

ROTATE BETWEEN SETS OF HASHTAGS

Let's say that you have a number of hashtags that have worked well for you, but you know that spamming your content repeatedly with them won't help. Within your niche, you can have a set of hashtags that you sparingly use for specific scenarios. You can have a set of hashtags for posts about your personal life, another set of hashtags for inspirational posts, and perhaps a set of hashtags for your ad shoutouts. This helps you tap into audiences based on search results and you can bring in more engagement to your page.

Ninja Hack: Have your hashtags saved in the notes section of your smartphone so all you have to do is simply copy and paste them into the comments section of your Instagram post.

DO SOME HASHTAG RESEARCH

Of course, all of the tips above are predicated on doing your due diligence in finding the right hashtags to use. A great tool to use is: SocialRank.com. It's free of charge and allows you to research the key hashtags being used by your successful competitors. You can also find the users that identify most with key terms and the most frequently used hashtags within each of those terms. There are other things you can do with Social Rank, but it really stands out as a great hashtag research tool.

Another great place to learn how to expand on your hashtags is: Hashtagify.me. Visit this website and learn how you can reach a broader audience on Instagram by finding hashtags that are similar to the ones you are currently using.

GEOTAG YOUR PHOTOS

This is a strategy I have not personally tested, but there are Instagram Influencers who swear that they have seen increased engagement on their posts from using geotags. Try it for yourself and see if it works for you.

Here, you are geotagging your Instagram photos as a way to add locality to your Instagram posts. I can see where this would be especially useful if you are a local business looking for exposure in your city or town, or operating in a niche involving multiple locations around the world. It turns out that more and more Instagram users are using "Places -> Near Current Location" in the search function. If your post is geotagged and they are searching for something in your niche, you have opened up the door to gain local organic traffic.

In conclusion, hashtags can definitely help you grow your Instagram following as well as act as a navigational tool for helping people find your content. Used correctly and sparingly hashtags will spread your content throughout the Instagram platform. Consider them to be icing on the cake – they are nice to have but your business or brand will not fail because you forgot to use hashtags or you use the incorrect ones. Make sure you have the fundamentals down pat before you start testing out different hashtag strategies.

CHAPTER 16

Turn Followers Into Buyers: How To Create Links That Produce Clicks

I f you take a look at any other social media platform, you have the ability to make your links clickable. When you enter the URL into your post, the link automatically becomes clickable and the website will usually open in a brand new tab or window.

With Instagram, you lose this privilege. Instagram does not currently allow users to post clickable links within a promotion/shoutout. You can ONLY host links in your bio – the profile of your Instagram page. Even then, you are limited in the number of links you can put in your bio. Because Instagram was not designed to rack up clicks, it is poor for clickbait purposes. Not to worry – this makes the interactions far more genuine.

It also makes things a bit harder on your end.

Fortunately, there is a way around this where you can still leverage your link and make your Instagram promotions work for you. This is where you'll need to drive traffic to your page and encourage Instagram users to click the link in your bio/profile so they can visit your website or sales funnel. Since you can't accept payments directly on Instagram, this is the most important part of the monetization process. Why? Because no clicks equals no money.

There are two ways to go about posting your link:

The first is to host the link in your own bio. You have to set up your bio in advance so that you can maximize the value that you get out of the traffic that is directed to your Instagram page.

Let's briefly recap how your Instagram profile should be structured for promoting a link in your bio: When writing your bio, start with the 'why'. This is where people learn what your brand is all about. Remember, it must be congruent with your promotion. Next, you want to highlight the benefits of the product you are promoting. People want to look at your page and see that your brand matches with the promotion that directed them to your page. Last but not least, you need to provide a crystal clear call-to-action that tells visitors EXACTLY what they will get when they click on your link.

You do not need to make your bio incredibly long (short bullet points works best). In fact, you will bury your link and reduce traffic to your website if your link is hidden at the bottom of a long bio. People should be able to see all of this information without having to scroll through your profile/bio. The link will be the last thing in your bio and it needs to be immediately visible.

The link should be something that's related to your brand name and your product, if possible, at the very least it needs to be related to your product. If you have a confidence product you are selling and the word "Confidence" is in the URL, that will drastically increase your click-through rate. Why? Because people will know exactly what they are getting when they click on that link.

The second strategy, and the far more powerful one, is to pay an Instagram Influencer to host the link of what you are promoting in THEIR bio. When you do this, make certain you have the link in your bio as well along with the exact same call-to-action the Instagram Influencer has. I've found that some Instagram Influencers don't like to put the link in their bios; and the ones who do will charge a slightly higher price for this. Pay the extra cash! Go the extra mile and have them do a promotion/shoutout where their followers will be told to click the link in THEIR bio. I have tested this numerous times, and I drive 3 times more traffic to my sales funnels when the Instagram Influencer posts the link in their bio.

Last but not least, make sure that you have software that can be used to track the link clicks. The problem with traditional tools like Google Analytics is that they can't always accurately track traffic where users clicks a link in an Instagram bio and then opens up in an entirely new window. You need something that provides an extra layer of tracking when it comes to your link clicks.

This is why I recommend Bit.ly, a free service that allows you to accurately track your link clicks. When you create an account with them, they let you easily track the amount of traffic you are receiving on your Instagram shoutouts/promotions. It's simple to set up, so you won't have to worry about a steep learning curve. You can track clicks from different Instagram Influencers and see which ones are driving the most traffic to your website or sales funnel.

I'll end this chapter with some metrics that are worth following for a link that is associated with a shoutout/promotion:

1. **Follower To Traffic Ratio (FTR):** This is the total amount of link clicks you get divided by total amount of followers of the Instagram Influencer. If you promote on a page with 100K followers and you get 100 people to your site, the FTR is 0.001. In general, FTR will provide you with a simple system that will show you what pages are good or bad, and therefore helps you see what Instagram Influencers you want to continue to work with. This will also show you how well your personal promotions perform. You can use software like ClickFunnels or Bit.ly to track how many clicks the link gets.

2. **Conversion Rates:** This is the total amount of opt ins or purchases divided by total traffic. For instance, if you drive 100 people to your sales funnel and you have 30 people opt in, that's a 30% conversion rate.

3. **Cost Per Visitor:** The total cost of a promotion divided by the amount of traffic/visitors to your website or sales funnel.

4. **Profit Multiplier:** The total revenue divided by the cost of the promotion. This one guides many of the decisions I make about how effective a given promotion was.

5. **Image/Caption Performance:** This is the amount of likes and comments for specific images and captions which equivalents into the overall engagement of this Instagram post or promotion.

6. **Date and Time:** The specific day of the week and time of the day a promotion gets posted. Different days suck and different days rock. For me, Fridays are historically the worst days and Sunday afternoons are my best. I track this to the minute and I always log the length of each of my promotions.

7. **Length of Promotion:** How many hours, days or months your promotion stays live.

I want to encourage you to keep track of these 7 metrics for every promotion you run and use a spreadsheet or some type of tracking system to document them. The points listed above will help you quickly evaluate how effective your promotions were. Soon enough you will have so much data that your shoutouts/promotions will become predictable and it will become simple to decipher if a partnership with an Instagram Influencer is worth the investment.

CHAPTER 17

Instagram Automation: How To Use Software That Takes The "Heavy Lifting" Out of Growing Your Page Without Risking Getting Your Account Banned

After you have mastered the strategies in this book, you can start thinking about automating your Instagram account. This can either add massive value to your business or brand on Instagram or ruin all the hard work that you have done up to this point.

There are dozens of software programs out there that plug into your Instagram account and automate your liking of Instagram user's posts, following and unfollowing Instagram users along with commenting. You program this software to engage with real Instagram accounts and it can dramatically increase your follower base along with drive a ton of traffic to the link in your bio, all on autopilot.

Virtually all the large Instagram Influencers use software like this. However, when you automate your Instagram account, you increase your chances of being banned temporarily or permanently by Instagram. You want to keep your follow and unfollow activity under 800 per day, and no more than 40 follows and/or unfollows per hour. You will want to keep your likes under 1,100 per day, and no more than 60 per hour. Automating commenting can be a bit tricky. Try to only use emojis and do not comment more than 110 times a day, and no more than 15 times an hour.

Always proceed on the side of caution when automating your Instagram account. You should know that the limits I just mentioned apply to Instagram accounts that have been around for awhile (2 months or longer). Violating the amount of actions (likes, comments, follows and unfollows) that Instagram allows its users to engage in per hour is a surefire way to get banned before you get started.

All Instagram accounts are under extra scrutiny when they are first opened. For this reason, you want to limit the use of third party applications that attempt to automate human activities such as the ones I just mentioned. (Automating DMs falls into this category as well) This doesn't mean you can't or shouldn't use automation software on your Instagram account within the first few days you open a new page. It simply means you need to tiptoe into the water.

You want to start off slow when you begin automating your Instagram account (300 likes per day, 500 follows and/or unfollows per day, do not use automated commenting at the beginning) and gradually build up your levels of automation. You would be well-advised to read Instagram's 'Terms of Service' regularly since they are constantly changing how many activities (likes, comments, follows and unfollows) accounts are allowed to engage in per hour. Also, if you are participating in engagement groups (like and comment groups) make sure automating your comments is turned off.

Automation software can be a game-changer. It can dramatically help you grow your follower base by thousands of real Instagram users on autopilot. However, like anything in life where there is a reward, there is always a risk.

I have personally tested virtually every automation software program on the market and there is only one that I have found to safely automate an Instagram users activity. It's call Instajam (GetInstajam.com). And it has helped me safely grow many of my Instagram accounts by 1,700 to 3,300 followers each month like clockwork. This is not an attempt to convince you to use automation software on your Instagram account, but rather to inform you that there is a legitimate way to grow your following without having to manually put in a lot of work.

One of the reasons why I like GetInstajam.com so much is because you are not using the software without professional guidance. The developers of Instajam regulate it and ensure that your activity stays within the regularly updated limits of the Instagram platform. With that being said, it is still your responsibility to know Instagram's Terms of Service before getting started with any automation software.

Here's how Instajam works: Your account will be pro-grammed to engage with real Instagram accounts that will become perfect prospects for the products and services you will be selling on Instagram. Liking, com-menting, following – all of that is safely done by the soft-ware. You get REAL followers from using this software, and not bots that will saturate your page and decrease the quality of your brand. If Instajam software follows an Instagram user for you and they do not follow you back within 24 hours, the software will automatically unfollow them. Why? Because the main objective is to increase your followers, and currently Instagram only allows you to follow 7,500 Instagram users.

When your Instagram account engages with other Instagram users it induces curiosity in the people who see that you have liked their post, commented on their post and/or followed their Instagram account. If you have set up your Instagram page exactly how I have instructed you to in this book, you will see that hyper-ac-tive followers in your niche are going to immediately follow you after Instajam engages with their Instagram account. Why? Because of something called the law of reciprocity.

"The law of reciprocity, (which applies in EVERY culture on the face of the earth), simply explains that when someone gives you some-thing you feel an obligation to give back. Giving and receiving favors is a common exchange and is an implicit assumption in most relationships."

The way the law of reciprocity works on Instagram is when you engage with an Instagram users account, they feel compelled to engage with yours. Why? Because when you do something nice for them such as like their post, comment on their post or follow them, they will want to do something nice for you. This typically results in them following your Instagram page and engaging with your posts.

The best part about this software is that you don't need to be online when it is automating your liking, following, unfollowing and commenting. GetInstajam.com is cloud-based software that will continue to grow your account while you are away from your phone. You could be in a meeting, sleeping, or playing with your children and Instajam will be hard at work growing your Instagram following for you.

Remember this: If you are using this software and you are not seeing lots of people follow you back (1,000 or more per month), it's likely the case that your Instagram profile and the content you are creating needs work. Reference chapter 4 and chapter 7 to ensure your Instagram page and the content you are creating is following the guidelines I laid out in those chapters.

You can check out this amazing software and see if it works as well for you as it has for me.

Disclaimer: I do have a vested interest in www.GetInstajam.com. I helped with the development of this software because I saw so many Instagram users using similar Instagram automation software and they were getting their accounts banned left and right.

What makes GetInstajam.com unique is that to date they have never had an account banned due to breaking

Instagram's Terms of Service. Something else that makes this software unique is the extraordinary amount of research that goes into targeting the perfect prospects that your Instagram account will be programmed to engage with. Instajam's automation software is constantly refining who your Instagram account interacts with. This constant refinement allows you to hone in and target people who will love your content and who will eventually become your customers or clients.

Many other similar softwares out there do not do any research at all and simply just program your account to engage with people who could careless about your content and will never buy your products and services. Other software programs on the market allow you to dangerously automate your Instagram account yourself.

If you're an expert in automation and have a deep understanding of where your perfect prospect is on Instagram and what their dreams and desires are, automating your Instagram account by yourself may work for you. But my experience suggests that most people will substantially increase their following and their bank account balances if they will leave programming their Instagram accounts to the professionals.

CHAPTER 18

Turning Followers Into Dollars Part 1: How To Create Digital Products To Sell On Instagram

Now that you have the fundamentals in place, you will get to see how this knowledge can be directly applied to selling digital products on Instagram. This is just one of the many ways through which you can monetize your Instagram page and create an additional stream of income or further grow your core business.

The Instagram-style sales funnel makes up a good portion of the selling process, but that is a topic that will be thoroughly covered in chapter 21.

First, let's discuss the benefits of creating a digital product. Why bother creating one in the first place? The reason is that you are providing value to your followers in exchange for a benefit that you will be receiving. You could be providing your followers a digital product to:

- Build an email list for an affiliate marketing product you want to promote, a digital product is a great vehicle for doing this.

- Generate leads and qualify prospects. They could be sent to a brief quiz to see if they would be a good fit for your business, product or service. A digital product as a reward for participating is a great way to increase the likelihood people will complete the quiz.

- Generate more traffic and set up an upsell offer. This is a great way to increase your profits utilizing a one-click upsell. (More on this later)

- Strengthen your email list. By providing more value through something like a free digital product, you are setting yourself up for greater sales success with a paid product to be released in the future.

One of the great things about digital products and digital courses is that Instagram provides you with an amazing platform for selling your knowledge. If you have unparalleled expertise in a field after thousands of hours of study, you can package that information into a product that people are willing to pay for. If you want to simply give some of your knowledge away, that can act as an attractive lead magnet or a freemium that leads people into your sales funnel where you can have a paid offer waiting.

Digital products allow you to quickly test new ideas with ease. Digital products can be easily modified and released as new versions with improvements and changes that will be beneficial to your customers. It doesn't cost a lot to make a digital product and they produce huge profits when they're combined with an effective Instagram Influencer promotion/shoutout strategy.

I've learned so much about selling digital products from taking dozens of online courses from the top experts in this field (Frank Kern, Vince Reed, Amy Porterfield, Eben Pagan, and more). I've also experienced my own success when I launched Instapro Academy.

Always keep in mind: Your prospects don't want digital products. Rather, they want two things: The results, and the RESULT of the result your digital products will give them. Sound confusing? It won't be when I explain the difference.

Let's say you created a digital fitness product. Your customer is looking for the RESULT of losing weight. That is the VALUE you provide to them and this result needs to be clearly communicated. The best digital product combined with a high-converting sales funnel won't help you make money if you don't articulate the results that your prospects will receive.

But what about the RESULT of the result? In the fitness example, what your prospect truly wants are esoteric things – increased confidence in all aspects of life, being able to play with their children without constantly finding themselves out of breath.

When do your prospects want results? Now! They want to save time with your solution. They don't have the time (or they don't think they have the time) and they are willing to pay someone who can help them shortcut their path to success (desired result). To really sell them on your product, you need to tie in the physical, mental and emotional results that they are going to receive.

Tony Robbins is famous for introducing the "Pain & Pleasure" model of motivation. Tony states that pain and pleasure are the twin forces of motivation. You use pain to help your prospective customers avoid something they don't want to happen, and pleasure to help them get something that they do what to happen.

Pain is twice as motivating as pleasure, so start your pitch with that. Identify your prospects deepest fears and use that to motivate them into taking action. After that, you have to get into the mind of your prospect and let them know about all the great things they can expect to experience in advance WHEN they get your digital product.

Your marketing message must be on point. It should clearly outline the benefits and the results your product provides. The best digital product in the world will suffer if a lousy salesperson is pitching it. The message must be carefully tailored to your customers needs and the quickest solution to their problem.

Make sure that you understand what your customer truly needs. You will have to be as empathetic as possible and learn to see things from your customers perspective. They need to know that you personally understand their situation and that you have the magic solution for them. Make sure your customers know that you have been where they have been and you know what needs to be done.

The more your customer feels that their NEEDS are understood, the more likely they are to keep reading your sales copy and eventually buy your digital product.

Finally, you need to have social proof of your product working in the real world. You need testimonials as proof that other people are able to take your product and get the results that your customer is looking for. With this credibility established, your customer is one step closer to clicking the buy button, and transferring money to your bank account!

Ninja Hack: Always put a testimonial next to the price of your product. This is extremely important if you are selling high-ticket digital products. People feel like they just got punched in the gut when they see that your product costs a lot of money. The testimonial absorbs some of that blow and reassures your customer that they are making the right decision.

Let's move on to the most important aspect of both your sales pitch and the design of your digital product: Specificity of a single result.

You need to stay focused on the ONE key result your client will get when they purchase your product. Always focus on the biggest NEED they have. It is important to keep things simple and avoid talking about the features of your product here. Your promotion should be engineered around the biggest need of the customer along with the one single result your digital product is going to give them.

The problem I see when people try to achieve too many results at once with their promotions/shoutouts is that their marketing message gets diluted and their prospect loses focus. When you're promoting your products on Instagram you don't have the time to educate people on multiple things at once.

You have to take your expertise and focus it around

achieving one result. You will not be able to create the perfect product that helps people with everything. I have personally tried this and it was my worst-performing digital product to date. Focus on ONE result and create separate digital products for the other results.

When you are able to describe the needs and desires of your prospects better than they can themselves, they will believe that you possess the solution to their problem(s). They will trust your solution and they will be eager to give you money to provide them with that solution. When they believe in you and your solution, you can give them the key to solving their pain point with minimal effort and time.

You want to keep this singular pain point in mind when you are creating your product (and the promotion for the product). The goal is to make it as easy as possible for the customer to follow along. If you provide a simple step-by-step framework that they can quickly use to achieve the end result, you have already succeeded. These steps need to make logical sense in order to get to the end result.

There are four questions that your customer will have in mind and your digital product needs to answer each of them without any ambiguity or confusion:

- WHY am I learning this? (Why do I need to know this?)

- WHAT am I going to get from this? (Every step is well-defined)

- HOW do I do this? (Step-by-step formula)

- What HAPPENS if I apply the information? (The end result they get)

Last but certainly not least, make sure that the name of your digital product is properly crafted. You are looking for something that is simple and self-explanatory. A customer should read it only once and know exactly what they are going to get. The easier it is to say, the better it works. When the same consonants or sounds are in the title, it becomes easier to pronounce.

How do you get started on making your own digital product? With regard to ebooks you generally have two options:

1. Make Your Digital Product From Scratch (the hard way)

If you are creating an ebook, you should be using Adobe Illustrator or InDesign which costs about $20 per month. This book won't be able to guide you through the entire process, but what you do is create several letter-sized artboards that serve as individual pages for your ebook. After setting up the perimeters and margins for each page through the use of guides, you draw text boxes into each page.

Using the pre-made content that you already created in a computer document, you paste them into the text boxes. I highly recommend that you do all of your writing on the document first because Adobe is not designed for typing.

You can also create your digital product using Google Docs and export it as a PDF to keep things more simple. I just started using this strategy and saved myself a ton of time but you do miss out on the design functionality of an Adobe product.

You can also throw in some lines at the end of each chapter for exercises that will help people reflect and take action on the material in your ebook. This provides more perceived value to the customer because your book allows your customer to interact with it.

If you are strapped for cash, this is the quickest and cheapest way I know for creating your own UNIQUE digital product.

As for your cover, there are two ways to go about it. The first choice involves creating your own book cover from scratch. You don't have to be a designer to align a nice-looking title, choose a fitting background, add your company name and use a stock image that is visually appealing.

The second choice involves outsourcing the cover design to services like 99Designs.com, Fiverr.com or Upwork.com. I personally recommend my friend Henry Kaminski at Unique Designz for affordable designs that will help you sell your book. (Remember: Covers sell NOT content)

2. USE PRIVATE LABEL RIGHTS (THE EASY WAY)

PLR products are pre-written books and ebooks that you can sell and keep all the profits. No catch – it's really that simple. The creators of these products have followed principles that are similar to the philosophies discussed earlier in this chapter.

If you are a coach on Instagram and you are looking for a free ebook to act as part of a sales funnel that leads to a coaching call, this is a great way to accelerate your success on Instagram.

If you are an affiliate marketer, you can give the book away to people in exchange for their email addresses. With your list built, you now have an audience that you can promote your affiliate products to.

Two websites to check out are PLRProducts.com and Master-Resale-Rights.com. Both of these websites are loaded with thousands of digital products you can use to attract your perfect prospects. They span across multiple categories and you are bound to find something that suits your niche.

Something important to note about PLR products: You need to inspect these products very carefully so that you understand what you can and can't market. In particular, Reseller Tools and Distribution Rights should be high on your list of things to look out for. You want to be able to resell a book, give it away for free or use it as a bonus item. You may even want the opportunity to alter some of the content if it is not suiting for your prospects. All of this can be found at the bottom of the page on the ebook or other private label right product you are considering purchasing.

You might not be a fan of the generic book cover designs that most of these books use, and so it would be helpful to see if you can make your own cover or outsource it to a designer (such as some of the ones I gave you just a few paragraphs ago).

Take the time to go through these PLR sites, create an account and see what is available. You want to check the reviews and the content of these books before you purchase them. They cost only $5 to $15 and are a very small investment for you and your Instagram business. If you don't like the digital products on the two websites I just mentioned, keep searching for other PLR sites until you find the right one for you and your niche.

If you are struggling to come up with a digital product idea, Clickbank.com is a great resource for looking at different products and how they are marketed. You can get EVERYTHING here. Each product comes with the name, the design, the headline, the sales copy, the email follow up sequence, the sales funnel – you name it, they have it on ClickBank.com.

After creating a free account on ClickBank.com, go to their "Marketplace" section and do a search with the "Gravity" filter turned on. This will generate the highest selling products for your search query, ranked from best to worst. When you see a top-ranked result, you know that people are buying that product and that it's in demand. Search for products within your niche, find the highest ranking ones, and learn more about the products to find out why they are selling so well.

You can get ideas about the color scheme that you should be using as well. An ebook cover design that you find on Clickbank might be particularly inspiring. You can look through different niches and get some ideas about how to create your own digital product.

Even if you have your own products to promote you can still use affiliate products as a way to increase your profits and improve your bottom line. (More on affiliate marketing in chapter 20)

There will be a link within each result on ClickBank to show you the backend resources that are available to you if you choose to be an affiliate for that particular product. Images, banners, sales copy, email copy, free bonuses, video sales letters, contests (for those with a large following) and so on. Some products will have more resources and some will have less. If you choose to promote the products on ClickBank.com and you don't like the graphics they provide you, you can always outsource them to one of the resources I gave you for designing your ebook cover as long as the affiliate manager allows this.

Just make certain that you are promoting high-quality products where you know exactly what is being sold. The last thing you want to do is to betray the trust of your followers and potentially your email list.

The best affiliate products on Clickbank are the ones that are mobile-friendly, offer a recurring billing option, and offer upsells. If those three things are in place in addition to what I just described above, you have a solid affiliate marketing product, or at the very least you have a tool that you can use as inspiration for creating your own products.

CHAPTER 19

Turning Followers Into Dollars Part 2: Selling Physical & Digital Products On Instagram

Instagram is an amazing platform for selling both digital and physical products and it still blows my mind how fast and how cheap you can drive traffic to your offers on this amazing platform. However, you will need to structure your shoutouts differently depending on what you are promoting. I have found that when I attempt to promote physical products the same way as I promote digital products my conversion rates are extremely low. In this chapter I want to discuss exactly how you should structure your shoutouts for both physical and digital products.

SELLING DIGITAL PRODUCTS ON INSTAGRAM

Photo: If you recall what you learned in chapter 11 about taking photos, your chief aim is to use physical pictures to promote your digital courses. You can take multiple images from several angles using different types of backgrounds and test them relentlessly to see what works best for you. This strategy has given me high rates of engagement and other high-profile users in my niche have experienced the same result. Your picture should not look like an 'ad' – rather, it should be a natural part of the Instagram environment. Remember to print out your digital ebook cover and tape it to a physical book or magazine cover. This gives it a look that seems 'real' and this technique has dramatically increased my conversions rates.

Caption: This is your headline and your sales letter. After your photo attracts them in, the caption will push them over the edge and convince them to click on the link in the Instagram page that is hosting your shoutout. You need to provide a compelling reason for them to visit your website or sales funnel, which will hopefully do the rest of the work for you. You need to tell people what the name of your product is and EXACTLY what they are going to get.

If you can, offer some FREE bonuses with your product. The word FREE on its own is an irresistible offer that will convert people on your website or sales funnel if it is set up properly. Don't hesitate to give them MORE reasons to click through and take action.

Always end with a dual call-to-action. You want people to visit your website AND follow your Instagram page. This strategy not only gets you sales, but it also gets you more followers. This is a two-pronged approach to selling digital products and it has worked amazing for me.

Make sure that you engage with the promotion/ shoutout. See what people are saying and reply back to them. By staying on top of comments, you can reply to questions, thereby establishing a connection and adding more value to the Instagram post. I've had a lot of direct sales come from this type of personal engagement with prospective clients and it has also helped me gain more followers!

SELLING PHYSICAL PRODUCTS ON INSTAGRAM

Photo: High-quality images are key to selling physical products on Instagram. I have seen a lot of brands dominating in terms of engagement rates and sales with their Instagram shoutouts for physical products. You want to have something unique about each picture. If you have a model, have them engage in an activity in the photo. Lifeless humans don't sell well! Try to have a background that is innovative and brings out the highlights of the product in the photo as well. Just like the digital product promotion, your picture should not look like an 'ad' – rather, it should be a natural part of the Instagram environment.

Caption: There are a couple of elements that make up an effective caption for a physical product. You don't need all of them, but it is helpful to include as many of them as possible. First, you want a description of the product in the photo that encourages a customer to buy along with the price. Next, you want to mention a discount if one is available. Flash sales, price reductions and free shipping are elements I always try to include in the captions of my shoutouts for physical products. These three things create a great sense of urgency and scarcity in the Instagram user's mind that makes them want to take advantage of these deals as quickly as possible. Instinctively, they know that they are only available for a limited time. If you are offering something for X% off, explicitly state this and provide the code that they can use to redeem their purchase.

Finally, include a call to action at the end that directs Instagram users to the link in the bio along with encouraging them to follow your Instagram page if you are promoting your physical product on and Instagram Influencers page.

An important component to selling physical and digital products on Instagram is leveraging the credibility of Instagram Influencers who already have large pre-built communities in the niche for the product you're trying to sell. Make certain you are structuring your shoutouts that promotes your product or service with a genuine recommendation from these Instagram Influencers. This is the most crucial aspect to leveraging the power of Instagram.

You don't want to go overboard and hype up the recommendation from the Instagram Influencer too much, but you do want to drive home the point that your product or service is personally endorsed by the Instagram page that is promoting it. The beautiful thing about Instagram is that people who follow certain Instagram pages look to these pages with celebrity status, and when a recommendation is made from one of these large Instagram pages the followers are extremely likely to take action: Buy your product or service, follow your Instagram page.

CHAPTER 20

Turning Followers Into Dollars Part 3: Affiliate Marketing, No Product, No Website, No Problem

Affiliate marketing is one of the best ways that you can increase your revenue on Instagram relatively quickly. Essentially, you are being paid to promote products that are created by other people. They have done all the leg work of setting up the website and the sales copy and all you have to do is to find these products and promote them to your followers.

In chapter 18 I mentioned Clickbank.com and I highly recommend you use that website as your source for finding high-converting affiliate products to offer to your Instagram followers. (More affiliate websites are listed in the Appendix of this book) You don't even need your own business or product to get started. People are making millions of dollars every day just by using affiliate marketing. When Instagram and affiliate marketing are combined, you leverage the full power of the hottest social media platform in the world.

Here's a more in-depth look at affiliate marketing and a breakdown of how the process works:

- Affiliate (you) posts an ad/shoutout for the affiliate product on your Instagram page (or on an Instagram Influencers page)

- Instagram user clicks on the link in the bio where they see the ad/shoutout

- Instagram user is sent to the affiliate website or sales funnel through your unique tracking link

- Instagram user makes a purchase on the affiliate website

- Affiliate records the purchase and the details of the transaction

- The purchase is confirmed by the merchant which validates the sale

- The transaction is credited to the referring affiliate (you)

- Affiliate (you) gets paid the commission (20% to 70% of the sale!)

This book has already taught you the formula for building a large Instagram following fast, now you can use your Instagram page to drive laser-targeted traffic to your affiliate offers and start making predictable profits. The best part about affiliate marketing is that all of the back-end aspects of the business` are already done for you. You don't have to deal with customer support issues or worry about bad reviews (Note: You should not be promoting products to your followers that have bad reviews) You simply just cash the checks the affiliate managers send you and move on to the next offer. It's impossible to run out of affiliate offers. There is literally tens of thousands of them out there.

For people who still can't get their mind around affiliate marketing, think about Amazon, a company that does more than a half a trillion dollars a year in business. In essence, Amazon is the world's largest affiliate marketer.

In my opinion, more Instagram user's should be using affiliate marketing to profit on Instagram. This is a huge untapped resource and I believe if you can find a way to generate consistent revenue on Instagram, then reinvest a portion of that revenue back into growing your following – that is a formula for massive long-term success.

Ninja Hack: One of the keys to having success when you promote an affiliate offer, is putting your personal opt-in page before an Instagram user goes to the affiliate offer. Instagram Influencer Jason Stone (aka Millionaire_Mentor) has been able to collect more than 350,000 email leads in only a year and a half by using this strategy.

Jason promotes all of his affiliate offers on Instagram and this has enabled him to grow an email list larger than many people who have been in the online marketing world for 20 years. I won't go into email marketing in this book, but you do need to know this: When you have a large email list; it could only be ten or twenty thousand subscribers, if your relationship is strong with your email list, you can pretty much print money on demand.

Affiliate marketing is an amazing opportunity for

anyone who builds an Instagram following. It not only gives them the opportunity to make substantial profits on a regular basis, it also allows them to collect email leads which – in my opinion, is the number one way to generate predictable profits.

Very few people know how powerful Instagram truly is. Few people understand how fast you can drive traffic, collect email leads, and make sales. But one of the main keys for people who do realize the power of Instagram is making absolutely certain their sales funnel is set up properly for the Instagram environment.

Let's dive in now and discuss how we can increase your profits on Instagram along with automating a process that will turn your Instagram page into a money making machine.

CHAPTER 21

The 8th Wonder of the World: Online Marketing Automation, Making Money While You Sleep (Sales Funnels)

This is the part where I get really serious about teaching you how to make money on Instagram. Whether you are selling a digital product or a physical product, promoting an affiliate offer or simply just offering a free ebook so you can collect emails for a later paid offer – sales funnels are going to be your best friend in this process.

What is a sales funnel? It's a multi-part system that is used to automate the process of selling your product or service. It is a series of pages integrated together so that when someone opts in, clicks a button or buys a product, they go to the next step in the funnel sequence. You can put anything you want in here including free content, paid content, recurring memberships – ANYTHING! You can put in upsells for high-ticket products and recurring services along with providing downsell options for those who would prefer to buy a lower ticket item. Upsells and downsells work great because you already have your prospects in a buying mode.

Sales funnels work for virtually any business; you can A/B test multiple options to see which funnel will work best for you and the Instagram strategy you pursue. Internet marketers are hopping on the sales funnel train as the best option for selling their products to potential customers and this does not appear to be slowing down anytime soon.

If you do not currently have a product or service you want to promote on Instagram, you can still use sales funnels to collect emails and build your list for a product you may have in the future. You can take the private label right products, perhaps one of the ebooks I mentioned in chapter 18 and use them as the bait to get people to your sales funnel.

Before I go any further, I want to recommend the ONE and only software that you will need for generating high-converting sales funnels in a short period of time: ClickFunnels.

ClickFunnels is a complete marketing software that allows you to easily build mobile-optimized sales fun-nels quickly and automate most of the selling process for your business. If you don't have a website set up or you're looking to upgrade your online presence, it might be the solution you need to convert the massive traffic you'll be driving on Instagram. Testing is extremely easy, you don't need any website building skills, it integrates with multiple third-party platforms, it's extremely simple in design and functionality, it's automatically mobile-optimized, and Clickfunnels comes with several pre-made high-converting sales funnel templates that will save you hours of time with design and development.

Whether you are a newcomer to the Internet Marketing world or a seasoned veteran looking to automate your online selling process, I promise you ClickFunnels is exactly what you have been looking for.

This book will not be able to walk you through all of the intricate details of creating your sales funnel, but what I can do is provide some general guidance along with some high-level strategies and most importantly, what you should and shouldn't do when it comes to launching your sales funnel.

First, I want to introduce the concept of splintering. This is where you take a product that is trying to do too many things at once and divide it up into several smaller products that you can use as separate parts of a sales funnel. A huge mistake I made in the beginning was trying to put EVERYTHING into a single product. You can't be everything to everyone, and I learned this when I noticed record-low conversion rates.

Instead, you can split things up and offer separate parts of your products as bonuses or even upsells in your sales funnel. Remember the lesson you learned from the chapter about product creation: You want people to achieve the SINGLE BIGGEST RESULT QUICKLY. Conveying the immediates results as well as the benefits the person who enters your sales funnel will receive is key to having a high-converting offer.

When I splintered my products and turned them

into multiple offers, I saw my profits rise significantly. I talked extensively about this in chapter 18 so this is just a friendly reminder to make sure you divide your products up into enough parts that will allow you to maximize each step in your sales funnel.

Let's go over some key elements that must be part of your Instagram-driven sales funnel:

- Mobile-Optimized: Your sales funnel MUST be easy to read on any mobile device.

- Clean Design + Quality: You are coming from a highly visual platform, so a high-quality design needs to be upheld throughout each of your sales funnel steps.

- Emotional + Logical: Solves an emotional pain point or provides emotional pleasure. And if you are offering an upsell it needs to make logical sense to purchase the item that's being sold in this funnel step. For example, if you are selling a copywriting product, a logical upsell would be a product about increasing traffic to the copywriting product.

- Use Pain + Pleasure: As you learned earlier, these are twin motivating forces of all human behavior. They must be present in each step of your sales funnel.

- Scarcity + Urgency: These two elements must be present in your sales funnel if you are going to convert visitors to buyers effectively and quickly.

Always keep in mind that you are referring traffic directly from Instagram. Generally, people don't want to spend a lot of money when they're going through a sales funnel for the first time unless your niche is well known for offering expensive products. Tread carefully and test to see what works for you and your ideal customers or clients.

There are numerous formats that you can use for your sales funnel. Regardless of which one you select, you need to have certain elements within each step of your sales funnel in order for the process to be effective. I will talk about exceptions to this as we go through each item.

RELEVANT AND ATTENTION GRABBING HEADLINE THAT ASKS A QUESTION

The question is one of the most important aspects. What you are doing here is causing a pattern interrupt in the prospect's thinking, this breaks their pattern of thought when they enter your sales funnel. You are going from a non-sales platform like Instagram directly to a sales environment. This question is designed to grab their attention and get them engaged and reading.

In terms of relevancy, people need to see your head-line and immediately know what they are getting. If you are selling a book, they need to know exactly what it is about and how it will BENEFIT them.

VIDEO SALES LETTER [VSL]

A lot of sales funnels are structured with a VSL that's placed directly in front of the person's eyes the moment they visit the initial page of the funnel. In most industries, a video sales letter provides higher conversions than a traditional sales letter due to the increased levels of engagement videos provide. This is something you will definitely have to test and see if this is the case for the sales funnel you develop for your product or service.

A VSL is just a long form sales letter put in the form of a video where each sentence is displayed one at a time and read out loud by somebody. They are usually no more than 4 to 5 minutes long, and you can always outsource the creation of it to someone on Fiverr or Upwork. You would just have to provide the pre-made sales script to the person you are outsourcing to.

On a mobile phone, a VSL will not automatically play. For this reason, you should put an arrow pointing down at the video with a statement like "Watch This Short Video Now to Learn The Secret" that will remind the person visiting your sales funnel to press play.

In rare cases you might not even need any more sales copy, the video alone could be enough to convince the person to purchase what you are selling. Nevertheless, the video might not always cut it. Let's move on to see what else we can include on the first page of your sales funnel.

A PICTURE OF YOUR PRODUCT

Remember how Instagram is a highly visual environment? The first page in your sales funnel has to be the same way. It should be a high-quality picture the clearly shows everything that is included in your initial offer. You also want congruency between your promotion on Instagram and all of your images found throughout your funnel so it is vital to pay close attention to every single aspect of your design.

A BUTTON THAT TAKES THEM TO THE ORDER PAGE

Within the button you want to put some captivating text ("YES! I WANT TO GET MY PRODUCTS AND FREE BONUSES RIGHT NOW") that will immediately take them to the order form where they can enter their credit card details or PayPal info.

You will want to have one "BUY BUTTON" immediately accessible when someone visits the first page in your sales funnel so that people don't have to scroll down to make the purchase. The longer your sales letter, the better it is to place several buy buttons to remind people at multiple points that they can make a purchase if they feel ready to do so. This is especially important when you think about how someone is interacting with your sales page on a mobile device. Too much scrolling can turn off a prospect who is ready to buy.

A COUNTDOWN CLOCK

Remember the principles of urgency and scarcity? There is nothing more representative of a limited time offer than a countdown clock that is slowly ticking away. People know that there's not much time left to act, so they better take action now! I've used countdown clocks on several of my funnels and it almost always provided me with higher conversion rates. ClickFunnels makes it super simple with just the click of a button and dragging over an element to add a countdown clock to your sales funnel.

EXPLAIN THE RESULTS THEY ARE GOING TO GET

People don't want your product – they want the BEN-EFITS AND RESULTS that your product is going to give them. This is where you really want to double down and write the most powerful and persuasive sales copy that you possibly can.

The best way to present these benefits is in the form of bullet points. People might not want to learn every detail about your product or service – all they really want is the BENEFITS AND RESULTS they will get when they purchase your product or service. In my opinion bullet points are the most effective way to clearly and quickly highlight the benefits and results your product will provide your prospects.

CREDIBILITY

If you are not an expert in your niche, don't worry! What you can do is borrow credibility from trusted authorities in your niche. University studies, scientific insights, statements from thought leaders – these are the elements you want on the initial page of your sales funnel. You don't even need to necessarily get a personal testimonial – you can simply paste quotes from experts that pertain to the importance of getting the key results that your product provides.

SOCIAL PROOF

There is nothing more convincing than seeing people who have tried your product and received the results that your reader is now eager to get. If someone else can do something, why can't they do the same thing?

You really want to make this section highly visual and personal. Have pictures of the people providing the testimonials and have them holding the physical product in their hands. For best results, make sure they are in an environment that highlights the product and are smiling showing they are enjoying the benefits the product provides. Place their testimonial right beside their picture and you have several more compelling reasons why your prospective customer should buy from you.

Video testimonials are not always easy to get. However, a video of someone describing the results they received from your product or service always produces the best results. The more emotional the person is in the video the more impact the testimonial will have on persuading a potential buyer to make the purchase.

MONEY BACK GUARANTEE

Offering a money back guarantee is something I've recently started doing and have seen great results so far. When people see that there is a 30-day money back guarantee on your product, that kills their emotional pain point of not being able to hit the delete button on their purchase. Simply mention that if they go through your product and receive no benefit, they can contact you within 30 days of purchase and they will receive a full refund.

The irony behind this is that I have had extremely low refund rates – 2% or less – when I use this strategy. Something I like to remind people in my video sales letters is: "If I can't make you money I don't deserve yours." Feel free to steal this phrase and use it for your own products and services. (I 'borrowed' the phrase initially from Russell Brunson)

As a side note, I don't just look at the guarantee as a marketing strategy but more as the right thing to do. My focus as a content creator is to provide value and ultimately results. If my digital products do not help someone get the results they desire I am more than happy to provide a full refund. If you embrace this same philosophy it will benefit you and your brand more than you could ever imagine in the long run.

DISQUALIFIER

This is a technique well known amongst Internet Marketers for increasing their conversions. You tell people that this program is NOT for everyone as a word of warning, and that they shouldn't waste their time if the product is not a good fit. You can even go further and provide a bullet point list of people who you think are not fit to be using your product. Paradoxically, this actually helps you sell more!

A REMINDER TO ACT NOW

Here's an example of this: *"You must act fast if you want to take advantage of this extremely limited time offer! Fill out the form below to get IMMEDIATE ACCESS right now for only $x before we SIGNIFICANTLY raise the price."*

You can put in some extra copy about how people will put off taking action forever and ever until the pain they receive from the problem they are trying to solve is excruciating, and by then it may be too late. Remind them in your sales copy that if they do this it will likely lead to them giving up and not getting any results. After all, it's the real action takers who will want to take immediate action and get the discounted price now instead of paying the full price later. This re-affirms the urgency and it creates a sense of action in the reader's mind because they don't want to think of themselves as lazy.

After you stack on a little pain make sure to re-confirm the money back guarantee and put another countdown timer here to instill extra urgency again.

A P.S. REMINDER ON THE BOTTOM OF THE PAGE

I've learned that people like to skim through the sales copy on the pages of my sales funnels without really reading it properly. No problem! I just put a small reminder at the very bottom of the page to remind them of what they missed out on. Here's an example of this:

"P.S. - If you are skimming through this and made it down here, we are offering a complete digital success program valued at well over $197 that could literally transform your life and help you create lasting success no matter what you are striving to achieve and we are giving it away ONLY to people who are dead serious about elevating their mindset, for only $57 today."

THE TWO-STEP ORDER FORM

Congrats! If your reader clicked one of the call-to-action buttons mentioned earlier or scrolled all the way down to the bottom and decided to make the purchase, you've come a long way. But don't relax just yet – we have another opportunity to provide an upsell that will increase your profits.

There are two steps to this small order form within the first page of your sales funnel. The first part involves the person visiting your funnel entering in some basic information such as their name, email and physical address. This is known as a micro-commitment. If you set this up properly in ClickFunnels prior to launching your sales funnel, you will have their email address automatically added to your list. This is crucial because in the event that the person does not complete their purchase, you can easily create an auto responder email that will send them a message to remind them about the great deal that they could be missing out on.

In the second part of the order form (step 2), you have the field where the visitor enters their credit card information. On this section appears a secret little tool that I like to call the "One Time Offer Box" which is an upsell on the first page that the reader encounters. Here, you can create a ONE TIME offer where you can add even more great content (additional training, an audio version of your product, reports, etc.) for a single payment that is typically higher than what they were initially purchasing. All the visitor has to do is click the box and it gets automatically added to their purchase.

Ninja Hack: You need to make it abundantly clear that this offer will NOT be available at any other time or place.

Once they choose not to add it on to their purchase, it's GONE FOREVER. See how we're coming back to the theme of urgency and scarcity?

It's really easy to create extra material for this upsell. As an example, you could record an audio version or a video course of your ebook and tack that onto it. From personal experience, this strategy has allowed me to surpass the original income I was getting from selling a single product alone without any upsells.

Now that we have covered what should be on the first page of your sales funnel, let's move on to the next pages in your funnel: The upsell and downsell pages along with the congratulations page.

THE UPSELL

The upsell page(s) can be one or more pages. It all depends on how you are structuring your offer and your sales funnel.

If the reader has made it this far, we have them in a buying mode. **A buyer is a buyer is a buyer.** We can keep selling them stuff (adding more value) if we structure the upsells in the right way. I've discovered that people are 8 times more likely to purchase an upsell once they purchased the initial product. You catch them in this very important moment and you leverage the fact that they are in a buying mood.

Order Progress Bar: I like to put this on top of the page and put a written reminder that their order is not complete. You will see a bar that is partially filled to visually show them how far they are in the funnel. Here is where the logical aspect of the sales funnel comes in. Your next offer needs to be something that makes logical sense to sell alongside the initial product. If you are going to use the upsell here to sell them more of what they originally purchased make sure it's an irresistible offer that gives them a deep discount. I've seen many online entrepreneurs have massive success using this strategy.

Example: The first bottle of skin cream they purchased on the initial page of your sales funnel sold for $19.95, now offer them 2 more bottles for $19.95. This increases their order at a significantly reduced price. Some will take this and some will not. But you never know unless you offer it.

Acknowledgement: In every step following the initial page, you always want to acknowledge their previous purchase. This allows them to follow along in the sequence and see how each purchase compliments their next one.

LOGICAL Upsell: If you have a copywriting product and your upsell is another copywriting product, your conversion rates for the upsell will probably be really low. But if you offer an upsell on increasing traffic to their new copywriting product they are going to be creating, that's something that would entice them to buy again.

Adding upsells to your sales funnel is key to increasing the dollar amount you can spend to acquire a customer. So get creative and do not only focus on selling one item in your funnel.

Some of the upsells that I have seen convert well consist of items like: Recurring monthly plans of a supplement that someone just bought, or a discounted price on multiple bottles of that supplement. Your upsell could be a comprehensive video course that expands on the principles taught in the ebook they purchased on the initial page of the funnel. Just make sure that it's a good fit and logical progression from the initial offer that they already purchased.

VSL: You can put in another video sales letter to show them the benefits of buying this new product or service. I always like to equip these with a reminder right underneath to "Order Now And Save 85% Off The Regular Price" (70% to 90% off works best based on my experience) along with an additional countdown timer. Make the timer 2 minutes or less to really put them in a state where they have to buy or miss out on an exclusive offer.

Cross Off The Original Price: A simple "Was $379, Now Only $79" will suffice. You want people to see that they are getting a significantly reduced price on what is going to be a relatively expensive product. For the best results, have a picture where the original number is visibly crossed off with a big fat red line. This is a play on psychology and it really strikes them as a great deal that they must take advantage of now or miss out on the deeply discounted price forever.

"No" Link or Button: This is the link or button that takes them to the next page of the funnel if they choose not to purchase the upsell they are seeing. It should take them to a downsell, or a page that congratulates them on their initial purchase. You want to use the right messaging in this link or in the button to make the person second-guess their decision.

Something like "No thanks, I'm not ready to create consistent and lasting results at this ridiculously low price" would work. See what that does? Nobody wants to click that and feel guilty for not wanting the benefit on that button or link.

On the upsell page you can incorporate some of the previous elements from the initial page in the sales funnel: A high-quality picture of the product, more of the benefits they are going to receive in a bullet point list, exactly what is included in the upsell, testimonials about the benefits people have received from the upsell, multiple call-to-action buttons (Send Me The Program NOW, YES! GIVE ME IMMEDIATE ACCESS).

Now, at this point there are usually three options: The person will be led to another upsell page, they will go to a page that congratulates them on their purchase, or they will be taken to a downsell page that is designed to convince them one last time to purchase a deal that they missed out on in a previous part of the funnel.

THE DOWNSELL

You can use more of the same elements that you used on the upsell page. You want to highlight how you understand that this product is not for everyone, yet you believe in them and you want to give them one last chance to get their hands on the product at a deep discount while they still can. Something I have been having success with on the downsell page is offering a 3 month payment plan for the item you were offering on the upsell page.

On the downsell page in the funnel I like to put in another progress bar showing their order is not complete, another countdown timer, a VSL, a picture of the product, the benefits they could miss out on, a few testimonials, a money back guarantee, and another 'No' link to give them one last opportunity to purchase the downsell.

CONGRATULATIONS PAGE

This should be the final page in your sales funnel and it should re-affirm the purchase(s) that they just made and display the links where they can access their product(s) if it is a digital product that can be immediately downloaded.

For security on your end, make sure that if there is a membership page that they can sign up on, they can only use the email that was used to make the purchase. That helps protect your products from being freely re-distributed.

On the confirmation/congratulations page you can tell them what is going to happen next and when they can expect to receive their product(s) if it needs to be mailed to them. This gives them reassurance that they are going to receive their product and that you are not leaving them hanging. This is a great way to build trust in the buyer, making them more likely to buy something that you will attempt to sell them in the future.

One of the benefits about ClickFunnels is that you have access to several high converting sales funnel templates that allow you to get multi-step funnels up and running in only a few minutes. ClickFunnels also allows you to easily build out online membership areas where your video content will be stored for your online training courses. If you use videos, you can privatize YouTube or Vimeo videos by making them unlisted and paste the private url into your membership area within ClickFunnels.

I've found that this is the most efficient way to upload videos and keep them secure.

Ninja hack: The congratulations page is also a ripe opportunity to sell an affiliate product. You can use a premade banner that will direct people to yet another product or service that will provide your customer with more value. Again, they are still in the buying mode even when they reach the last step of your funnel!

You can sell your products while receiving affiliate commission at the same time. Just make sure that the product is logically related to your initial purchase like the upsell product(s) was.

There are an unlimited amount of ways that you can design your sales funnels. And there are numerous objectives that you can achieve with your sales funnels. For the purpose of Instagram, I recommend you focus on the ones listed below:

- Collecting emails
- Marketing affiliate products
- Offering free ebooks, reports, audios or videos
- Selling digital or physical products
- Providing free plus shipping offers
- Qualifying people for your coaching and consulting services
- Collecting leads and qualify prospects for a high-ticket offer
- Getting people to register for your webinar

No matter what your marketing objective is, your

Instagram-driven sales funnel can do it for you effectively if you design and develop it the right way.

Generally, there are three types of sales funnels that I use when I'm promoting my products on Instagram. Don't take these as something set in stone – these are very basic templates to give you an idea of how sales funnels function and also to provide you with an outline and a little inspiration for when you sit down and build out your first funnel.

OPT-IN FUNNEL

Purpose: Building An Email List (for your own products or affiliate products)

1.   Free Value (Ebook, report, case study, video, access to the next thing)

2.   Upsell/Apply (Next thing, maximize, better, faster, application, qualify)

3.   Confirmation (Confirm, direct, access, affiliate offer)

DIGITAL PRODUCT FUNNEL

Purpose: Selling Digital Products - Upsells, Maximizers and Membership Programs

1.   Direct Offer (Ebook, course, audio) [$4.95-$7]

2.   Maximizer (Bonuses, maximize, better, faster) [$27-$97]

3.   Upsell (Next thing, maximize, better, faster, trial offer) [$197-$397]

4.   Confirmation (Confirm, direct, access, affiliate offer)

FREE + SHIPPING FUNNEL

Purpose: Selling Physical or Digital Products - Upsells, Maximizers and Membership Programs

1.   Free + Shipping (Book, audio, DVDs, product) [$7.95-$12.95] <- Buyer pays shipping only

2.   Maximizer (More, bonuses, maximize, better, faster) [$27-$77]

3.   Upsell (Next thing, maximize, better, faster, trial offer) [$97-$297]

4.   Confirmation (Confirm, direct, access, affiliate offer)

When you are creating a sales funnel for Instagram, the key is simplicity. Listed below are the elements I recommend you include in your Instagram-fueled sales funnel:

- **High-quality image of what you are selling in physical form:** If you are selling a digital product, it will drastically increase your conversions if you put a crisp image of the product in physical form on the top of the initial page of your funnel. Remember when I mentioned earlier in the book the strategy I used that involved printing off the digital ebook cover and taping it to a physical book? That is exactly what you should do.

- **Captivating headline:** You want to provide the benefit of the benefit. If you sell a fitness product, the benefit is that they lose weight. The benefit of the benefit is increased energy and confidence. Here's an example: "You're About To Discover A Foolproof, Science Based Method That's 100% Guaranteed To Melt Away 12 to 23 Pounds of Fat In Just 21 Days." The key here is to get them to take action. Additionally, make the headline a moderate size so that your mobile users can read the entire headline the moment they see the initial page of your sales funnel.

- **Call-to-action:** "Simply fill out the short form below and get instant access now". This is asking for information prior to the offer or the free bonus that they are going to receive. This gives them direction and implies that the process will be very easy. You want to stage several calls to action throughout your sales funnel to give the visitor multiple opportunities to take action.

- **Two boxes for name and email:** "Enter Your First Name Here" and "Enter Your Email Address Here" will suffice. Again, we want to give people simple directions.

- **Engaging buttons:** "YES! GIVE ME ACCESS NOW!" would be a good example.

- **Promise of security:** Remind people that the process is 100% secure and that you will never share or sell their information to anybody.

Always remember: When people are sent to your sales funnel from Instagram, everything needs to be congruent – the branding, the product layout, the sales copy and the colors and fonts that are used throughout.

Sales funnels are the magic ingredient that helps people turn their Instagram pages into money making machines. But probably the most overlooked benefit of using sales funnels on Instagram is the fact that you can build a massive email list FAST!

When you're building an email list on Instagram you need to provide Instagram users with an incentive that will encourage them to share their email with you. Free content is the best way I know to achieve this objective. When people are giving you their email address, they are looking for an exchange of value. A free ebook that teaches them how to do something or solve a problem is of high value to most people. Ebooks are extremely inexpensive. You can purchase ebooks for virtually any niche on private label rights websites like: www.Master-Resale-Rights.com for as little as $5 and give them away in exchange for an Instagram users email address.

When you're promoting your ebook on Instagram, you want to have your caption do a great job of framing the benefits and compelling people to visit the mobile-optimized sales funnel that has your opt-in page ready. Focus on the benefits your ebook will provide an Instagram user along with a personal endorsement or recommendation by an Instagram Influencer if you are using them to promote your ebook. Always be certain to close the caption with a call to action directing the Instagram user to click the link in the bio as well as follow your Instagram page if you are not promoting your ebook on your own page. Review the principles I taught you in chapter 14 ("How To Write Captions That Get Your Followers To Take ACTION") of this book to get the best results possible.

Once your email list begins to grow, this is an excellent

opportunity to provide more value to your Instagram followers and make sales. What I like to do with my email list is offer two value-based emails (no offer) followed by an email that has an offer. This could be an offer to purchase one of your products or an affiliate product you are selling. I typically send my value-based content out on Monday morning and then again on Tuesday morning. Then Wednesday around lunchtime I send an email with my offer. I pretty much just rinse and repeat this strategy every week.

Many of the email platforms that marketers use integrate directly with ClickFunnels and ClickFunnels even has their own email platform (Actionetics), so don't worry about entering any data or dealing with a difficult setup.

If you want a book that goes into great detail about growing your email list along with developing amazing sales funnels, I highly recommend that you check out "Dotcom Secrets" by Russell Brunson along with the sales funnel that he uses to sell the book. This book teaches you about dozens of sales funnels, email sequences, successful headlines, the best baits to attract your dream customers, and reverse engineering tips for hacking your competitor's sales funnels.

The best part about building out your sales funnels is that you don't have to include every single element that I talked about earlier. You can choose to leave some of them out or use more of them depending on what's appropriate for your niche and what gets you the best results.

Some industries will require that you include additional information on your sales funnels for maximum effectiveness as well as to meet regulatory requirements.

For example, if you are selling a health supplement, putting in FAQ's addressing the reader's concerns and a medical disclaimer would be in your best interest.

Don't forget about the trigger words that I described earlier: "Free" and "Bonuses" work just as well in sales funnels as they do on Instagram promotions and advertisements.

Last but not least: Do not forget about the concept of MODELLING. Russell Brunson talks indepth about this in his book Dotcom Secrets. I'd like to share some of his insights with you before I conclude this chapter.

Russell had to learn the hard way that the best way to succeed in online marketing was to use what was already working for other successful marketers. He realized that it was a waste of time to learn how to build your own sales funnels from scratch when you could simply model what others were already having success with.

His first time-saving tip was to find DIRECT competitors – people selling the SAME thing as you are in the SAME market. Brunson suggests that if competitors do not already exist in your market, then it is probably in your best interest to not enter that market at all. The reason for this is because there is most likely not enough demand for your product or service.

Once you find a successful direct competitor, you are going to want to model them, not COPY them – there's a big difference and you don't want a lawsuit over your head. Your first version should look similar to theirs in terms of the layout – you want to mimic the feel that their overall design and copy provides to the person entering their sales funnel.

When you are modeling other people's sales funnels it is important that you go through each and every step of their funnel – all the upsells and the downsells. Russell Brunson took this to the next level and took screenshots as he was going through each step of his competitors sales funnel, and he even eventually bought his competitors products so he knew exactly what they were doing. Russell would copy out the VSLs word for word.

No matter what his personal opinion was, he knew that if his competitors were making millions, they must be doing a lot of things right. You can imagine that this was his only option since his competitors weren't just going to hand their million dollar funnel over to him. (Note: To take this a step further, I recommend you make a special folder for all the email follow ups that will be sent after you purchase the products of your competitor's in their sales funnel.)

All you want to do in your market is leverage what other people have already successfully done. You want to look at the EXACT pricing strategies that people use (not your own clever variation) and use that. When people try to get creative in their pricing, they lose. Why would you want to use anything besides the price points that have already been tested and proven to be successful?

Once you stop trying to be innovative with your funnels and stick to the tried and true methods that work, then you can begin split testing other variations to see what converts the best. Try new headlines and button colors to see how that affects your conversions.

Just make certain that before you come up with your own variations you have already reverse engineered every single part of your competitor's sales funnel (and email follow up sequence) and figured out what's working for them. In Russell's case, he only had to spent $100 to go through each step of his competitors sales funnel and find out exactly what his competitors were doing.

ClickFunnels makes it super simple to do split testing. You don't have to go through the laborious process of creating a new funnel from scratch. With one click you can simply duplicate your page and swap out a headline or change a button color to see how that affects your conversions. As people go through your funnel and buy your products, ClickFunnels automatically tracks conversions and lets you know which funnel variation performs best.

This was a very basic overview of sales funnels and how they can be leveraged to maximize your profits on Instagram.

Always remember, imperfect action always beats not taking action at all. When you first begin creating your sales funnel keep it simple and find what works best for you. Don't let the "how" hold you back from taking action. I'd rather you have a good strategy implemented than a great strategy that takes so long to put together that it never gets put into action.

Start small and improve. Continue to analyze and adjust. Understand that sales funnels can automate your entire selling process. Sales funnels will enable you to spend more time doing the things you love while still allowing you to provide the lifestyle you deserve.

CONCLUSION

Turn Advertising Into Wealth

Throughout this book, I've provided you with a lot of tips, strategies and actionable advice. It may seem like a lot initially if you read through this entire book in one sitting, so I highly encourage you to go back, review each chapter carefully and implement each strategy you learned. Work on one technique at a time until you've mastered it, then move on to the next.

As I mentioned at the beginning of this book you cannot do the fancy stuff without mastering the fundamentals first. When it comes to mastering the fundamentals on Instagram, everyone will have their own strengths and weaknesses. Maybe you need to work on networking with Instagram Influencers to build up a relationship where they feel comfortable personally endorsing your products and services. Perhaps you need to work on creating eye-catching images that stops an Instagram user from scrolling through their newsfeed and engages with your post. It is important that you focus on areas that need improvement because the only way you will have massive success on Instagram is if you combine each of the strategies you learned in this book and consistently apply them.

Never forget that the Instagram game is a continuous hustle. At the beginning you will have to put in an extraordinary amount of effort to gain momentum. You will have to promote the same objective on the same Instagram page multiple times a week. I've discovered that it takes several exposures before people are convinced that they want to buy your product, download your ebook or possibly follow your page.

The most important thing here is to not allow the lack of initial results to discourage you. Keep going and continue to test as many strategies as you possibly can. Test different images for the same promotion, test different captions, test using unique hashtags, test different Instagram Influencers, test the time of day when you run ads and always A/B test your sales funnels.

Keep testing all possible combinations until you hit the sweet spot. You'll start to see things kick into overdrive when you are consistently reaching at least 2 million people with your ad shoutouts. I know it may sound expensive to reach that size of an audience, but it's really not. It's very easy and affordable to get your products and services in front of millions of people on Instagram. I can easily accomplish this for only $200.

One of the beautiful things about being able to reach such a large audience so quickly is that you're able to get immediate feedback on your marketing strategies.

That's why it's never been easier to rapidly test numerous techniques until you find what works for you. Adaptations can be made in an instant and you never have to worry about having to wait several weeks until you can try something new. You know how your promotion performs right away, which allows you to make changes instantaneously.

Instagram has opened up a world of opportunity that I didn't think was possible.

And despite being a lifelong entrepreneur, I had to relearn many lessons about success and persistence because of all the obstacles and challenges I went through when I was building my business on Instagram. It was an experience that humbled me and taught me many new things about the world of online marketing. I'm incredibly grateful for all of the setbacks, and there isn't a single moment that I'd change. Now I consider the valuable lessons I've learned such a blessing, that I felt it was my obligation, and duty to share them with you.

Understand that although I've done everything possible to help reduce the amount of trial and error you will go through, as you begin to implement the steps I've outlined in this book you may encounter some of the same setbacks as I did. There may be times when certain strategies do not work out the way you expect them to. For example, there might be a shoutout that does not generate the amount of followers or traffic you anticipated or maybe there will be a few Instagram posts that do not get you the level of engagement you would have liked.

Do not let temporary setbacks stifle your momentum. Stay focused on your end goal, the purpose for which you are utilizing Instagram, and keep in mind that failed promotions are nothing more than lessons learned. Continue to take action, analyze and adjust the results you get and consistently apply the techniques you learned throughout this book. If you are able to do that, I have complete confidence that you will be able to overcome any obstacles that come your way as you're growing your following and finding ways to profit on Instagram.

Always remember that Instagram is a platform that is continuously expanding and things will inevitably change as they continue to grow. Stay aware of new opportunities that arise and always look to expand on the strategies that you learned throughout this book. The more time and energy you invest into learning and eventually mastering Instagram, the sooner you will see results and discover new and more powerful ways to grow your business effectively on this amazing social media platform.

You now have the exact, step-by-step blueprint for creating massive success on Instagram. You know exactly what it takes to turn your Instagram page into a powerhouse brand that delivers valuable content to an engaged community. But most importantly, you now know how to market and advertise your business on Instagram successfully, and as the legendary marketer Frank Kern says, "The most dependable and consistent way to generate wealth is to turn advertising into profit."

The plan for turning advertising into profit on Instagram has been given to you throughout this book. Now it's up to you to take action and implement it.

Jeremy McGilvrey

ACKNOWLEDGEMENTS

When I think about all the people who have supported me and made sacrifices in their own lives so I could do the things I love like write this book – it plants a lump in my throat and tears in my eyes.

Therefore, the amount of people I have to thank is immeasurable. But I would first like to thank my Lord and Savior Jesus Christ for dying for my sins. Second, I want to thank my father Mike McGilvrey for sticking by me during some of the most difficult times in my life. Next, I want to thank my love Nerissa for tolerating my ridiculous obsession with constantly pursuing my dreams. I can't tell you how much it means to me honey when you don't get upset when I get out of bed at 3 o'clock in the morning and rush to my office because I have an idea that I'm so excited about I just can't sleep anymore.

I want to thank my newborn son Tristan for helping me realize how magical the miracle of life truly is. I want to think my son Thomas for providing me with more motivation than anyone on this planet. Thomas, everything I have and everything I will become was made possible because of you. And not a single day goes by that I don't think about you and whisper that I love you.

I want to thank Peter Beshay for believing in me and allowing me the opportunity to be apart of his vision.

I want to thank the co-founder of ClickFunnels Russell Brunson for opening my eyes to a world that I did not realize existed. Tim Johnson, Peter Lazidis and Keri Scruggs are three people I have to thank for walking in my life when everyone else walked out. I want to thank my grandmother Karel Shults for the character traits that you planted in me during my childhood years. Those traits have paid enormous dividends throughout my life.

Lastly, I want to thank Jason Stone. Jason you changed my life...seriously. I was a struggling Internet entrepreneur before I met you. Now I'm one of the top experts in the world for teaching business owners how to position their products and services online allowing them to go from brick and mortar to click and order.

ABOUT THE AUTHOR

Jeremy McGilvrey lives by the mantra that you don't get what you deserve in life, you get what you work for. He believes that thinking life is fair is akin to thinking a bull will not charge you because you're a vegetarian. And his all-time favorite quote comes from the book How the Mighty Fall by Jim Collins:

"The signature of the truly great versus the merely successful is not the absence of difficulty, but the ability to come back from setbacks, even cataclysmic catastrophes – stronger than before. Great nations can decline and recover. Great companies can fall and recover. Great social institutions can fall and recover. And great individuals can fall and recover. As long as you never get entirely knocked out of the game, there always remains hope."

Jeremy is someone who pours his heart and soul into everything he does. Ingrained deep in his DNA is a ferocious drive and the trait of either being all-in or being all out. There is no in between with him. Few people can have an effect on other's like Jeremy does. If you spend more than 5 minutes with him you will quickly be infected by his passion and zeal for life. Understanding where his chutzpah comes from is something many people are yet to discover. But most people who know Jeremy know this: His ability to breakdown complex problems into simple solutions is second to none.

The love Jeremy has for his family is what constantly has him in pursuit of making a difference in this world. He tries hard everyday because it's extremely important to Jeremy that he leaves a legacy behind that his children will be proud of.

In Jeremy's spare time he works. Not because he has to, but because there's few things he would rather be doing than finding ways to test out new marketing strategies and improve conversions on his sales funnels. He is obsessed with getting the tiniest details right in everything that he does. That's why Jeremy is currently one of the most sought after marketers in the world for helping business owners capitalize on the massive opportunity the Internet offers.

APPENDIX/RESOURCES:
Valuable Instagram Tools

ANALYTICS

Social Blade

Iconosquare

Social Rank

MESSAGING

GroupMe

Kik

Telegram

WhatsApp

PHOTO EDITING

DarkRoom

WordSwag

AdobePost

Canva

Word Dream

TextOnPhoto

Snapnote

Phonto

Typorama

ROYALTY FREE IMAGES

Pexels.com

Unsplash.com

FreeImages.com

SALES FUNNELS

ClickFunnels

Unbounce

LeadPages

OptimizePress

AFFILIATE MARKETING

Clickbank

JVZoo

MunchEye

LINK CREATION & TRACKING

Bit.ly

ClickMeter

LinkTrack

SHARING

Buffer

IFTTT

BACKING CONTENT UP

Google Drive

Dropbox

Evernote

DOWNLOADING PHOTOS & VIDEOS FROM INSTAGRAM

InstaDownloader

InsSave

PLR PRODUCTS

PLRProducts.com

Master-Resale-Rights.com

PRODUCT CREATION

Adobe Illustrator

Audacity (free audio software to record audio)

Camtasia

ScreenFlow

OUTSOURCING (Design work or content creation)

Upwork

Fiverr

99Designs

INSTAPRO ACADEMY

www.InstaproAcademy.com

"Instapro Academy shows you the exact strategies all of us big Instagrammers are using to grow our following and make huge profits on this amazing social media platform. That's why Instapro Academy is my No. 1 recommended Instagram training course."

Jason Stone, Millionaire Mentor

"When God puts a dream in your heart, when He puts a promise on the inside of you, He deposits in you everything you need to accomplish that dream. He doesn't give you the desire without giving you the ability."

Joel Osteen, Pastor Lakewood Church

Made in the USA
San Bernardino, CA
13 December 2017